JUST

> *In this book, Ed Cronin brings unique experience and perspective on domestic and international policing. Through a first-hand account, Ed addresses issues that many in policing have faced throughout time. I highly recommend this book for people who need to understand the complexity of crime.*
> - Edward Davis, Former Boston Police Commissioner and International Security Consultant

> *Ed's story from when he went through the Police Academy, was a cop on the beat, and then progressed through the ranks to Chief of Police is a gripping one. He deftly paints a picture of the most prominent events that shaped his life and his work. You, as the reader, can actually picture the dank police headquarters with the paint chipping. The most significant takeaways from the stories that are interwoven reveal how Ed demonstrates empathy, deep listening, respect, and true leadership with everyone whom he encounters. He is a leader who is extremely humble. There are some gripping moments that present themselves to Ed which make him reflect and ask questions of himself about racial justice. You seriously will not be able to put this book down as you read about the family dynamics that shape Ed, to finally being accepted by fellow police officers for the impact he has made on the international level.*

- Dr. Carol Ann Sharicz is a professor, author and consultant specializing in systems thinking and leadership. To date, Carol has done work in 15 countries including Australia, Belarus, Belgium, Brazil, Canada, China, England, India, Estonia, Germany, The Netherlands, Hong Kong, Japan, Moldova, Russia.

America is currently at a dark moment in policing. Author Ed Cronin shines a light on the pathway to betterment with **Just Policing**, *his own riveting story of growing and evolving in police work, in handling domestic abuse, in assisting with international police training, and in his work with the U.S. State Department. This book clearly shows the changes within U.S. policing over the past 40 years, steps both forward and backward. It also reveals how the best of American policing can have an important positive effect on policing in Eastern Europe - Ukraine, Russia, Moldova - which, in turn, can affect America's national security. Such an important topic comes to life as a page-turner that you can't put down! Not only does this book help the reader to understand how America arrived at this state of inequality, but it supplies the most important ingredient: A hopeful roadmap with multiple solutions for more effective policing.*

- Liah Kraft-Kristaine, J.D., former attorney, bestselling author, executive and author consultant, and Executive Director of Life Star Academy Foundation for girls without families who are aging out of U.S. foster care.

JUST POLICING

MY JOURNEY TO POLICE REFORM

Edward F. Cronin
with
Dayna M. Kendall

Copyright 2022 by Edward F Cronin
All rights reserved. No part of this book may be reproduced without written permission from the author except by a reviewer who may quote brief passages or reproduce illustrations in a review; nor may any part of this book be reproduced, stored in a retrieval system, or transmitted in any form or by any means electronic, mechanical, photocopying, recording, or other form, without written permission from the author.
This book is manufactured in the United States of America.

Dedication

For Sue,
My love and partner

Dear Claire,
Thank you for your support and all the love you have brought to so many,
Ed Cronin

Acknowledgements

  Writing this book has been a very long process that began several years ago. It wasn't until I met and talked with my co-author, Dayna Kendall, that this book finally came to life. She was instrumental in helping me to tell my story by her inquisitive and articulate questioning and editing that allowed me not only to write my story but also to affirm my reasons for doing so. I will always be grateful for her critical input and countless meetings in coffee shops.

  So much has combined in my experiences, education, direction, opportunities, and inspiration that have coalesced to result in the knowledge and perspectives that I have brought to this book. I want to acknowledge with gratitude some key factors in what has shaped and developed me. Special thanks to the following:

  To my University of Massachusetts professor and department chair of the Criminal Justice Program, Dr. Eve Buzawa. Dr. Buzawa's exceptional programming, knowledge, and expertise in the field of criminal justice inspired me to develop critical thinking skills that have served me so well over a thirty-plus-year career in the field of law enforcement, both in the United States and in the international arena.

  To all my friends and colleagues at Project Harmony in Waitsfield, Vermont, especially to Renee Berrian for her always strong and uplifting support, and to Director Charlie Hosford for having confidence and encouraging me to grow professionally on many levels.

To my former Fitchburg Police Department supervisor, Captain Joseph Carbone, who quietly mentored, encouraged and guided me to develop the skills that I would use as a police officer over the course of my career.

To attorney Ed Ryan, outstanding trial lawyer, civil rights activist, and former President of the Massachusetts Bar Association for his critical assistance in my appointment to become a police officer and for supporting and assuring my appointment as chief of police in Fitchburg.

To systems thinking Expert, author and Professor, Dr. Carol Sharicz, who introduced me to the concept and work of systems thinking and applying it to my work as police chief. Using systems thinking analysis resulted in reduced crime and an award by the International Chiefs of Police Association to me for the work that was done at the Fitchburg Police Department: Thank you, Carol!

To my dear friend and author, Board Chair of Moon Jaguar Strategies and Chief Restorative Practitioner, Sayra Pinto, MFA, PhD, who reached out to me when I was Chief of Police in Fitchburg. She encouraged me to look within through self-reflection to understand the tragic consequences of systemic racism and apply methods that would end the cycle of violence and crime in my city.

To my daughter, Jessica, whose birth, love, presence, and enjoyment in my life has sustained me and inspired me to lead a life of growth and support of others. To my stepchildren, Aaron and Cicely, who have contributed so much love to their families and communities. I am so proud!

Finally, to my wife, Susan, who has been by my side for 37 years, always patiently supporting and sacrificing for my work, whether it was hosting and caring for citizens of my local community or for international figures in other countries. I could not have done any of this without her love and selflessness.

Table of Contents

Acknowledgements 6
Foreword 11
CHAPTER 1   Epiphany:
A Christmas Nightmare 16
CHAPTER 2   Growing Up:
Sorting through Bedlam 28
CHAPTER 3   Learning Policing:
The Real Story 44
CHAPTER 4   UMASS Lowell:
Putting in the Extra Effort 59
CHAPTER 5   Learning the Job:
Trying to Organize Chaos 69
CHAPTER 6   Oxford:
What I Thought I Knew 83
CHAPTER 7   Russia:
Shock and Awe 93
CHAPTER 8   Gardner Police:
Careful What You Ask For 109
My Photographic Journey 128
CHAPTER 9   Project Harmony:
Taking It to the International Community 138
CHAPTER 10   Return to Fitchburg:
Executing the Plan 149
CHAPTER 11   Bag Job:
Or Who Stole My Cheese! 159
CHAPTER 12   Sayra and Systems:
Finally, There was Hope! 169
CHAPTER 13   Searching for Answers:
Unexpected Results 182

CHAPTER 14   In the Shadows:
Negotiating the Pain 195
CHAPTER 15   A Virus Takes Leave:
Back to the International Arena 205
CHAPTER 16   My Stay at The Lodge:
More Success for Fitchburg 219
CHAPTER 17   Moldovan Life and Politics:
Proving Myself Again! 229
CHAPTER 18   The Plan and the Mission:
From Corruption to Success! 242
CHAPTER 19   Just Police Reforms:
History Tells Us So! 255
About Edward F. Cronin 266
About Dayna Kendall 269

Foreword

  Forewords are the parts of the front matter of a book that tell the reader why they should read this book. I think you should read this book because I had goosebumps the entire time that I read it.

  It tells the story of a man who taught me, over four years, the difference between the police in Honduras and what the police can be in the United States. It tells the story of a struggle for belonging that is shared across communities. It is a foretelling of the America that is to come if we unite together and ground ourselves in the deep appreciation of our humanity, across differences, and as we take full responsibility for our power and our communities.

  Since my four years of working alongside Ed, and because of those years, I have developed a deep commitment to American institutions. There are people who made a civil service vow and who endeavor every day to honor it. And yet, within our institutions, there are active poltergeists, ghosts of the past that incarnate today to continue to perpetrate harm. For that reason, I am certain that there are still many broken hearts at the core of our institutions.

  I met Ed Cronin at the tail end of a troubled and violent experience on the streets of Chelsea, Massachusetts, where I worked with local gang members to change patterns of systemic and gang violence and learned about police corruption first-hand. When I think about what Ed and I accomplished together in the short span of four years, I am both amazed and grateful. This book tells the story of what

America can be: A land where laws, votes, relationships and visions count.

As an immigrant from Honduras, I grew up understanding that the police could not be trusted because they committed all types of crimes with complete impunity. Often linked to military and paramilitary personnel, the police were in a separate category that could do no wrong. The militarization of police and their entrenchment in the protection of US corporate interests often resulted in people protesting social and economic injustice only to have their efforts and their lives swiftly snuffed out by well-armed military/police/security personnel.

Justice never arrived for those aggrieved, and many police/military/security perpetrators of this violence continued to live their lives with no consequences. A contemporary and poignant example of this overlap between military/police/security and corporate interests working in unison was the execution of Goldman Prize winner and Honduran environmental Lenca activist Berta Cáceres on March 2nd, 2016. Six years later, little has been done to hold those responsible for her execution accountable although it is widely known that her name was on a kill list developed by former US-trained elite military groups in the Honduran army.

As I worked countless hours to decrease gang recruitment trends and to neutralize gang violence in Chelsea, I was aghast at the number of stories that were shared with me about the participation of gang unit members in the distribution of drugs and guns through specific gangs in the city. Gang wars were incited to cover up this small but intense system of corruption led largely by some individual cops who were in collusion with gang leaders. I actually did not want to believe what I was hearing about that until the day we attempted to hold a peace circle between the local MS-13 and the Bloods in our neighborhoods.

About 20 of us had gathered at Quigley Park one summer evening and as we were about to begin our circle, a police wagon descended upon the park. Everyone, including my staff, were made to get on their bellies. I was told to stand aside and watch the proceedings. The leader of the Bloods was extricated from our group and locked up in the wagon. I was later told that he had stopped trafficking the guns and drugs folks had been "misplacing" from the evidence locker in the police department and that the results of his act of insubordination was a sudden discovery of ten "dime bags" in this kids' jeans pocket, and two years of lock up for him.

After my tenure was done in Chelsea, I ended up taking a job in Leominster, Massachusetts, at Mount Wachusett Community College. The various regional educational institutions had partnered with the local Latino community to create a strategic plan to improve the educational outcomes for local Latino students. The regional Latino community leaders had asked me to come to support this effort.

As I prepared to begin my tenure at the college, I methodically met with every institutional leader who was a part of that collaboration. When I saw that the Fitchburg Police Department was a leading partner in this effort, my heart went cold. I had no interest in actually partnering with the police. The trauma of my Chelsea experience was fresh and much on my mind.

Despite my concerns and reluctance, I went ahead and asked for a meeting with Fitchburg Police

Chief Cronin. I showed up fully intending to be polite, with no expectation of any significant exchange. I was ready to tip my hat, endure the usual condescending commentary about my community, and to keep going through my day.

Ed must have had a hard day that day. I later found out about the police brutality cases he was managing and the intensity of the murder rate in his city. He made a comment out of frustration that was something like, "What is wrong with the men in your community?!"

I froze and quickly saw that I was at a crossroads; one path would likely lead to my firing, and the other led to complete subjugation. I chose the former. I had been fired before, several times. I also had quit and had been trashed for it. So, I really had nothing to lose. I quickly responded by saying, "What is wrong with you? You are the one with the cars and the guns and the power."

I just remember the pause between us. A deep silence. I held my breath and opened my eyes a little wider because I just wanted to shut them down and wait for the avalanche of blowback that would come my way for having spoken my mind. Instead, Ed looked at me, held his gaze and said, "Thank you for talking back at me. I have never had anyone in your community actually respond to me."

I let out a deep breath of gratitude and elation. "Could it be that I actually could talk to this man?" I thought to myself. My eyes widened even more out of anticipation and hope. "Can I actually work with this man?" I asked myself in utter disbelief.

Many years later, Ed's impact on the City of Fitchburg is felt even today. Considering the many solutions that are so needed right now, his work should reach a nationwide audience. What outcomes and evolution could occur in communities if police and government officials were actually interested in learning from leaders like Ed, who serve small suburban regions where relationships still ground the lives of communities? Instead of lifting up only big coastal city police chiefs, what if law enforcement in cities and towns of all sizes actually wanted to learn from places that are the most common in our society? Then I believe Ed's story and ideas will be highly relevant to all communities, a teaching tool in the creation of the America that will belong to all of us.

Sayra Pinto, MFA, PhD
Chief Practitioner, Moon Jaguar Strategies
Board Chair, Gathering Power

March 10, 2022

Chapter 1

Epiphany: A Christmas Nightmare

Christmas morning 2002 arrived dark and cold in north central Massachusetts. I was sound asleep when the phone rang at 4 AM. I was accustomed to hearing my phone ring at all hours of the night, but on this particular morning, I hoped that the call was for any reason other than work.

Groggy, I raised the phone to my ear. My hopes were dashed as I heard, "Good morning, Chief." It was Sgt. Ernie Martineau, the officer in charge at the police station, and the man who would one day be chief of police.

"I'm sorry to do this to you, but I knew you'd want to know," he continued. "We had a double murder last night, and we got a third person just barely hanging on."

"I'm on my way," I replied, hanging up the phone.

The adrenaline rush from this information prevented me from putting my head back on the pillow. I felt my blood begin to pump as I lifted myself from bed and began to dress in the shadowy, pre-dawn, careful not to rouse my sleeping wife.

The car crunched along icy roads as I drove, finally reaching the rear of the police station. The station's bright lights pierced the deep purple sky. I was no longer sleepy. The knot in my stomach grew tighter, reminiscent of my high school football days in the moment just before the first snap of the game. I did not know what was going to happen, but I knew it was game time as I walked up to the door.

As I entered the station through the rear glass door, I was immediately aware of a heightened level of professional urgency going on around me and felt a sense of pride in my department. This force was where I had cut my teeth as a patrolman in 1980, where I had worked for over fifteen years, rising through the ranks to the role of detective sergeant. Some seven years later, I had returned to take over as chief.

As I entered the report room area with its badly stained rug, scuffed up woodwork, and fixed computer area, I noted a flurry of activity. One officer was typing away at his keyboard, unaware of the blood on the back of his fingers on his left hand. This officer had been to the murder scene and had not yet had a chance to get washed. Another officer walked by quickly with a handful of papers.

After speaking to the officer in charge, I left the operational area and went up to the next floor of the station that housed the detective bureau and administrative offices, including my own. Dark fluorescent light shone down on me while climbing the stairs to the second floor. From there I walked straight down the empty hall to my office, unlocked the door and put on the lights.

The stark stillness of the office gave me pause as I let myself acknowledge what an empty place this was to be spending Christmas morning. I watched as other detectives assigned to investigate last night's murders were slowly trickling into the bureau. The first detective I saw was the detective supervisor, Phil Kearns, one of the most temperate and professional officers I have ever worked with. He later became a police chief as well.

I asked him where the others were. He said that they, too, were on their way into the station, many having to explain why on this, of all days, that they had to leave their loved ones. It was on mornings like these that we all became intimately aware of how much we gave up to serve our community.

I wanted to contribute to the effort going on. "Is there anything I can do?" I asked Kearns.

"I'm all set for now," he said.

I realized that no one had found the time to make a fresh pot of coffee, an addition that would be appreciated by all. It felt like the least I could do.

A short while later, as I was turning on my computer, the detective supervisor stood in my doorway. "I just realized that there is something else you could do to help."

"What would be good?" More than happy to take something off his plate, I was ready to handle whatever my department needed.

Kearns gestured towards the lobby with a nod of his head. "We have some family members of the victims in the lobby. They've been here for quite a while. Could you speak with them?"

I knew the challenges he would be facing and that he was working hard to get up to speed, considering the overwhelming tasks that lay ahead. He would have to respond to the crime scene to process evidence and take lengthy interview statements from victims and witnesses. I went down the side stairs near my office to the lobby where I observed three Latinas, one older and the other two in their late teens who turned out to be sisters and the daughters of the mother. All the women appeared exhausted and wore pained looks on their faces. I knew that this was no place they wanted to be on a good day, let alone on Christmas morning. I felt compelled to reach out to this family, to listen to their story, and to lend the dignity of my office to the words they had to say.

I invited them to come with me. All four of us climbed the stairs to the second floor and continued in strained silence as we walked down the dim hall, retracing the path I had just walked a short time ago. I showed them into an interview room near the detective bureau.

In the past, I had witnessed many different reactions when families learned of the death of a loved one. My memory flashed quickly back to an incident involving a man who had committed suicide in his own home. His adult son had come home to the scene and was told by an officer what had happened to his father. When the veteran officer I was working with, Jack Murray Jr., who later became the Ashby police chief, notified the son of his father's death, the son immediately swung a hard punch and struck the officer flush on the jaw.

My instinctive reflex had been to jump in to defend my fellow officer, but the assaulted officer had held me back. His eyes caught mine, and he cautiously urged, "No, Eddy. Don't. Don't do anything."

The officer turned away from me, and turned towards his assailant, quietly consoling the bereaved son. The son continued to yell in anger before dissolving into tears. That noble act by my fellow officer was the inspiration that I needed at this moment.

The interview room lighting was soft yet faint, and the space served as an all-purpose area. This was the very room where I had made coffee in a gesture of goodwill earlier. This room had hosted numerous detective meetings and provided a private space for difficult conversations. The furnishings were dated, with worn-out industrial gray carpet and institutional light oak chairs with stained red cushions on the seats and back. My head and heart felt simultaneously heavy. This meeting took on a gravity that was not lost on me in that chaotic moment.

A deep tension existed between the Latino people in our city, the third largest in Worcester County, and the community at large. It always seemed that the only attention this population received in our newspapers was negative. This othering, this so-called treatment of residents in my own city bothered me to my core. New to the role of chief, I felt it incumbent upon me to model for my city a means of engaging this population with kindness, respect, and humanity.

In this meeting, I would be the lone representative of a community that had historically degraded and disregarded the culture of the women sitting before me. Against this backdrop, I sensed the tension that both the mother and daughters felt. I watched as the mother folded and refolded her hands in her lap, and my eyes were drawn to the blood on her hands, like the officer downstairs typing his report.

I immediately realized that they, too, had both been to the murder scene. My officer downstairs was trained to navigate such a tragedy, but these women had seen a sight that no civilian should have to endure.

A movement in the hallway prevented my eyes from lingering too long on her bloodstained hands and disrupted my train of thought. I saw the unmistakable silhouette of Jose, a strapping six-foot plus Latino officer with broad shoulders and the smile of a little boy. I excused myself from the women for a moment to chat with Jose. I had invited him to join me when speaking to the family. I knew I did not understand this culture well enough at a time of such tragedy and Jose could serve as a bridge to help me pick up on any cultural cues that I might miss.

I returned to the interview room with Jose towering outside the door. Taking my seat across the table from the mother and daughters, I asked what I could do for them. The mother did not speak English and one of the daughters served as the interpreter. They were all very shaken and upset. The daughter told me that her mother wanted to know what happened to her son. I told them that I would find out.

I found myself leaving the room yet again, breathing deeply as I walked across the detective bureau to the supervisor's office after getting her son's name. I then asked Phil, "She's asking what's going on with her son?"

The sergeant looked at me blankly and told me, "Chief, he's dead."

I took a breath. "Well, don't you think we should tell them?" He agreed.

As I re-entered the interview room, I could see the anticipation in the faces awaiting me. The mood in the room was somber as I returned to my seat across from the women.

Reinforcing my voice with a tone of professionalism, I began to speak to the daughter who was interpreting for the mother. "I don't know how to tell you this, but her son is dead."

Despite the language barrier, this mother knew exactly what I had said before her daughter had the chance to repeat my words. Upon hearing the news, the eyes of the mother in front of me shuttered and squeezed tightly closed. I was unprepared for the reaction that came next. Both the mother and the daughters began to wail loudly. The scene had gone from tense professionalism to wildly out of control. Screaming in Spanish for a telephone, the bereaved mother ran out into the detective bureau, reaching for a phone on a desk with her blood-stained fingers. Her actions caught me completely off guard.

I felt a sense of embarrassment for the women's public display of their painful emotions. It reminded me of my days walking the beat early in my career when I had seen a mother in a similar plight respond in the same way as the women before me now.

The mother in front of me suddenly dropped to the floor of the detective bureau and was now rolling around on it, shrieking and crying, in a convulsion of agony. I saw it as a patrolman, and I saw it now as a chief.

Feeling a sense of responsibility for the raw suffering in front of me, I wondered silently to myself, and then aloud to Jose, "Is there anything I could have done differently?"

His eyes caught mine as he said, "No, Chief. You have to let it go."

His soft words registered hard on my psyche. I had done the best I could in this impossible situation. But something continued to gnaw at my insides. Perhaps it was a tinge of guilt, or maybe worse. How could I accept the unexpected grief response of a white man hitting my fellow officer upon finding out that his father was dead by his own hand, and yet I was embarrassed by a mother grieving the loss of her son after a brutal murder? These responses were one and the same - the human expression of catastrophic loss and trauma.

I found myself wanting to retreat, a deep-seated need to run and hide from this overwhelming situation, but I knew that I had no choice but to be still with these feelings. And I had to restore the calm in this chaos. Gently, Jose and I were able to guide the mother up from the floor and bring both mother and daughter back into the interview room as the other daughter silently put her arms around her mother.

They appeared to have started to collect themselves as they found their way back to the same seats that they had previously occupied at the table. They were all sobbing quietly, something that I could identify with and which seemed like a more appropriate public expression of grief to me. Their more tempered response felt safer because it was familiar. It was how I, as a white, French and Irish Catholic man, had learned how grief should look. Who was I to judge another person's expression of loss, and how foolish was I to believe that people had to grieve according to my own experience? I wanted to be open to learning how others experienced grief, but there was no time to indulge in processing what I had just experienced.

As I was trying to collect myself enough to leave the room, the commander of the state police detectives, who had ultimate jurisdiction of this criminal case, appeared in the doorway of the interview room. I could only imagine what he was thinking, but it was likely somewhere along the lines of "What the hell is going on here?"

I politely introduced him to the mourning women seated across from me, and I attempted to explain his role to them.

The commander spoke sharply. "Chief, can I talk to you alone for a minute?"

We walked a short distance into the detective bureau, away from the women in the interview room. The commander looked at me with a very concerned expression. "Chief, I really wish you hadn't done that -- hadn't talked to those people."

I was perplexed. He must have seen the confusion or the dismay evident on my face.

He clarified, "They didn't need to know he was dead. We could have split them up first. Got their stories, you know? That really would have helped us to conduct this investigation more efficiently."

There was no question in my mind that the commander was insinuating that I had dropped the ball, and his message was a not-so-subtle inference that I better not have fucked this up. Again, I felt my insides bottom out. His words to me about splitting up the family to interview them sounded so wrong and hollow. In light of all the anguish that had just taken place, didn't this family deserve better?

My thoughts were with the victims, their relatives, my city, and my police department. This was affecting everyone. Being new in my position and having just recently returned to the policing scene in Fitchburg, I chose not to respond to the commander's statement. Instead, I walked away, stunned by his words, and what felt to me like a challenge to my moral authority as chief of police in Fitchburg, Massachusetts.

My priority upon taking this job was to answer the urgent need to show a compassionate, caring face to my city that had been deeply suffering from open wounds. I was rusty in my cop instincts, and I found that I was somewhat disappointed in myself for not responding to the commander more aggressively. But I knew that walking away and not engaging was the right thing to do, a sign of growth beyond my days of shooting from the hip and acting on pure instinct. Policing required one set of skills; leading the police required a different set of skills. I was also coming to realize that I needed more time to process what this all meant. I knew in my heart that giving precedence to processing a crime scene over establishing communication with a victim's family was the wrong approach.

"How on Earth did things get this way?" I wondered to myself. I did not think that my colleague from the state police was asking for anything other than to ensure that a new police chief was making absolutely certain that proper procedure took place during this investigation. A serious crime had been committed, and the commander was responsible for the resulting investigation, but it felt like no one was considering the big picture here. I couldn't help but think: what would have happened if this murder had occurred to a prominent white family in my community? Would I have allowed a prominent white family to be split up and be interviewed before I had been able to inform them of their loved one's death?

This double murder on that day involved a Latino family, and, in fact, most of the murders occurring in the city in 2002 were Latinos killing other Latinos. There was no doubt that this murder was being treated as an investigation but something about the way we responded to this violent event did not sit well with me.

Having spoken with one of the victim's family and with the commander, my job for the day was essentially done. The police detectives were in the building, setting up at their desks to do their work. The investigation was underway, and I felt it was time for me to leave. I exited the building the same way I had entered and saw one of my dispatchers outside having a cigarette break.

As I passed by, I shook my head in disbelief, saying something to him about how senseless and tragic this all seemed.

He stopped me and said with a smile, "But, Chief! It's still Christmas!"

I paused for a moment and half-smiled. "Thanks, Bobby. You're right. Merry Christmas," I said as I shook his hand and headed towards my car.

I started my vehicle, turning on the heat to combat the chill that I felt coursing through my body. The overcast morning was barely any brighter than it had been when I had arrived at the station several hours before. I pulled out and started my short ride towards home, a home where my family was warm, safe, and was still intact.

The ground was blanketed by newly fallen snow that formed a thin crust as vehicles traversed the road. My car never seemed to warm up enough to stop me from shaking. Bobby was right. It was still Christmas Day and I needed to get home to prepare with my family.

The ride home was dominated by a shocking numbness, almost as if I wouldn't allow myself to have any coherent thoughts. I just felt an overwhelming sense of relief to be out of that intense activity. As I pulled into the driveway, our Christmas lights sparkling and twinkling against the gray, cold morning focused my attention. It was a different type of game time now, as I coached myself to pull my act together.

As I opened the door to the house, the warmth and smells of Christmas emanated from inside, and I was overcome by a wave of something different. Whereas my ride home was characterized by numbness, now in the safety of my own home, I was able to let down my guard.

My wife met me near the front door with her usual stoic and compassionate embrace. Despite the fact that my face must have said it all, she still asked, "How are you doing"?

I embraced my wife and let out a deep sigh. The shock of my first major crisis as chief had just occurred. I felt this burden on my shoulders and asked myself, "What are you going to do about it?"

Chapter 2

Growing Up: Sorting through Bedlam

After a traumatic Christmas, I could not help but think back on another visit I had made to the Fitchburg Police Department. But in that instance, I was the one under arrest. My late teens and early twenties found me drowning in alcohol. What initially began as a release, an opportunity to indulge in fun and let loose, resulted in escapist behavior and a complete dependence on alcohol. With my judgment impaired, the decision to start a street fight after a night of boozing seemed to make complete sense, until I was picked up by two patrolmen on the midnight shift.

Unimpressed by my macho, alcohol-fueled antics, they cuffed and stuffed me like I was a rag doll and threw me in the back of their cruiser. The inside of the cell block where I was detained was no place I ever wanted to see again. I had been pushed through a big black iron door with Wells Fargo stamped on it, dating from the 1890s. I then saw two tiers of a metal cell block with decades of black chipping paint on its bars. Neither the deplorable conditions of the cells, nor the embarrassment of my drunken state bothered me.

But it was seeing my mother's face as she walked into the cell block to post my bail that caused in me a feeling of shame that I never forgot. I made a promise to myself at that moment, despite not yet being able to quit drinking, that I never wanted to put my mother in a position of being disappointed in me again.

My mother, Alice, had been a source of tender love and affection for me in an otherwise chaotic household. I was one of seven, not an uncommon occurrence in Irish Catholic families in those days. My mother's calm demeanor and spiritual devotion was in sharp contrast to my father, Tom, a violent man contending with his own demons.

A soldier and prisoner of war during World War II, my father suffered from what is now widely acknowledged as post-traumatic stress disorder (PTSD) from his experiences. My father had been captured by Hitler's Afrika corps and was transported to a prison camp in Italy where he was abused and starved to near death. He had escaped his captors no less than six times, each time returning to unthinkably brutal prison camp conditions, until he finally was successful. And that success required jumping from a vent hole on a moving train.

He was being transported to Germany to another prison camp after the Italians surrendered to the Allies. The jump resulted in a large open cut on his face that left him with a jagged scar be bore as an everyday reminder when he looked in the mirror.

Upon arriving home from Europe, an invisible war continued to rage on within my father. Knowing what I later learned through policing and from my own research and work in the field of domestic violence, I came to understand how this trauma kept my father hopelessly frozen in the past, perpetually on edge, awaiting the next impending threat. He seemed incapable of experiencing joy for himself or witnessing it in others.

I have a visceral memory of being slapped upside the head anytime I laughed too loudly or reveled in any form of delight. As an adult, during some of my happiest moments, I found myself nearly flinching as I was conditioned to expect the blunt trauma to my skull that would accompany these kinds of emotions.

My relationship with my father was deeply conflicted. I was equal parts terrified of my father's erratic behavior and yet strangely proud of him for what he endured as a sacrifice for his country. Even more heart wrenching as a child was watching in frustration and anger as my mother bore the brunt of his wrath. There is no doubt that my childhood created deep-seated anxiety and trauma in me and my siblings, but it was my mother who endured the worst of the physical and psychological abuse.

My earliest memory of my childhood was from when I was about four years old. My mother was gone. I remember looking out the window of our house yearning for her. It felt as though my mother had been away for a long period of time, what seemed like several months to me, although I don't know how long it really was. Missing my mother was a regular occurrence in my youth. From my earliest memories to the time I was seven or eight years old, my mom would disappear from time to time, and my siblings and I were split up to live with relatives. Thinking back, I remember being told that my mom was in the hospital without ever fully understanding what ailed her. I just knew that I missed her with an ache in my heart that made it difficult to breathe.

My mother always treated me in a special way, which made her periodic absences even more difficult to endure. The closeness I felt to her was a lifeline in the midst of my intense, often chaotic upbringing. She introduced me to my faith in God, and even though we had little of material value, she always tried to instill in me a spirit of adventure and excitement to enrich my boyhood.

I remember sitting on a bed with my mother at the age of five learning how to sew buttons on my shirt. She was so kind and patient with me and always gentle and understanding when I made mistakes. Whether it was standing up my green bean "soldiers" in my mashed potatoes or telling me that I could be anything I wanted to be when I grew up, she always left me feeling that I was special. Her tender heart was on full display one day when I was studying the photograph of a boy who looked identical to me. It was a photo of a boy standing in the front yard of our house wearing jeans and a t-shirt.

I pointed to the image before me and exclaimed to my mother, "That's me!"

My mother gently corrected me, saying "No, sweetheart. That is a picture of your oldest brother, Tommy."

I looked again in disbelief as he was the spitting image of me. Tommy, named after my father, was my mother's first-born son and my eldest brother. It was the winter when Tommy was five that he had been sledding down the driveway on the side of our house. Tommy was hit by an oil truck and was killed.

Only as I grew into an adult did these puzzle pieces of my childhood finally fit together. It seems obvious now that my close resemblance to my dead brother was probably both a curse and a blessing to my mother. It explains why, with such a large family, she always took time to nurture me and to see to my happiness. It also explains my mother's sad moments, the times when she was gone for long periods when I longed for her warmth and compassion. Never did I understand these absences or the reasons for her hospitalizations until I learned that my father blamed my mother for the death of my brother. Furthermore, my dad refused to let my mother grieve Tommy's death.

My life in catholic school paralleled my life at home as I endured a mixture of both blessings and horrors. Many of the nuns who were responsible for my religious education were like my mother. Their teachings laid the groundwork for my understanding of spiritual sacrifice and compassion: to feel for those less fortunate and take actions to help them. Those lessons would later lead me to dedicate my life to the best aspects of police work.

But in stark contrast to the actions of these gentle sisters were the behavior of the nuns who, like my father at home, ruled their classrooms with intimidation and physical violence. I have vivid memories of a 36-inch wooden ruler exploding into pieces after slamming off the backside of a fellow classmate whose sin was watching a discussion between the nun and another student. He was beaten for "Not minding his own business," as the nun explained.

I could never forget the torment of one pathological nun who used to slap us each on the open hand with a ruler as we lined up to use the boy's room in the morning. She said that we were being punished for things we would do during the day that she did not see. I was not a troublesome student and would only get a light tap while the boys who were viewed as problems took the hard blows.

These kinds of bizarre and cruel behaviors combined with the violence and bullying of the school yard made grammar school a nightmare, compounding the trauma. I will never forget being teased by older kids and crying to the point of exhaustion where tears would no longer fall. Neither home nor school provided the escape I needed from witnessing and experiencing the terror of violent beatings that shook me to my core.

What should have been a safe place to learn would become an explosive mental minefield that sent so many mixed messages to me as a young child. It was later pointed out to me by a therapist that my desire to be a police officer was probably rooted in having the ability to right wrongs but also to be able to create the order that was missing in my upbringing.

During my elementary school days, I was a good student, probably in the top 10% in my class. I was able to succeed and learn despite a class size of fifty students in one classroom. Even though there were many downsides to attending catholic school, I am grateful for all the passion and excitement that many of the sisters put in to bring the materials alive on the pages of the books I studied. I will never forget opening my geography book and studying a page about Russia and looking at a *babushka* with a worn face and a scarf on her head with endless fields of wheat behind her. This photo was alive for me and made meaningful through the nun's teaching of the subject. I thought, "I want to go there someday." Little did I know at the time how true that wish would become.

I was able to focus on my schoolwork and avoid the notoriety that other boys drew. In fact, my demeanor drew a different type of attention. When I was in third grade, a kind nun asked me one morning what I had for breakfast. I told her that I did not eat breakfast. In a time that predated free breakfast in schools, this nun arranged for me to have bread and butter and milk every morning.

Later in life, I saw this as a wonderful and generous act of kindness, and I realized that she recognized that I needed this sustenance to learn. She was filling a crucial need in my growth and learning, teaching me about the type of person that I wanted to become.

The time had come to move onto high school. My first choice was to attend a local college prep school, Notre Dame High School, located in Fitchburg. I watched my older brother, Michael, attend this all-male school taught by an order of religious brothers. I loved listening to him talk about his participation in the debate club and his stories about playing high school football. This was enough to convince me that I wanted to follow in his footsteps.

Around that time, I had been asked by my parish priest where I was going to go to high school. I told him that I wanted to go to Notre Dame, but I did not think my parents could afford it. He told me that he would get me in. I don't remember discussing this again after the school year ended. In my mind, I was going to follow Mike and be just like him.

I wanted to begin my freshman year and play football. I scoured the sports section in the newspaper every day to find out when summer football practice began at Notre Dame. I finally found the August start date, signed up, and drew football equipment at the high school to participate in double sessions practices. I remember the heat, sweating, and pain of two practices a day for two full weeks before school began on the Tuesday after Labor Day.

I showed up to the first day of school excited yet uncertain of what awaited me. There was much clamoring in the hall with students and teachers walking in every direction. A loud bell caught my attention and I watched as everyone quickly dispersed. Not knowing where I was supposed to go, I headed towards the office in the main lobby. I told the kind woman seated at the front desk who I was and asked her where I should go. She checked a list and then stood up to leave the room. A moment later a man came in and told me that the school had no record of me and that I did not belong there.

Feeling the blood rush to my face, I left the office in a stunned silence. I remember little from my walk home, but I do know that I was able to hold back my tears until I saw my mom and told her what happened. No one was looking out for me, and no one was guiding me. The debacle at Notre Dame gave me a glimpse of what it felt like to be excluded. I had the sense that the people who were in charge, the parish priest, even my mother, had things to worry about other than me. I found myself starting 9th grade at a brand-new school called Veterans Memorial Junior High School.

This was my first day ever attending a public school and it was a bit overwhelming at first. I adjusted quickly and soon found that I actually began to like it. Unexpected solace came with learning that the school had a ninth-grade football team. After going through two grueling weeks of summer practice with the Notre Dame team, I was well ahead of most kids going out for the football team.

Football became a safe place for me, one where I could channel my aggression and feel a sense of accomplishment on a daily basis. The coaches constantly urged my teammates and me to dig deeper within ourselves to excel. This was a lesson that I would never forget. But it was because of football that I had one of my most traumatic moments in school.

The incident took place at lunch time. Elbow to elbow, my friends and I sat eating our lunch in the cafeteria, talking about the day. Sitting at the end of the table was a young classmate of mine who was totally blind. A fellow football player sat down next to the blind boy and knocked over his milk and began laughing at the scene. This incident humiliated my blind friend and enraged me at the same time. I stood up in a fit of anger, prepared to defend my friend, and told the football player that I was going to kick his ass after school that day.

In my anger and loss of temper I failed to take into account that he was much bigger than me and that I had committed myself to a challenge that I was not sure would end in my favor. Word quickly spread throughout the school that this fight was going to take place. A small group surrounded my opponent and me when we stepped out behind the school. At this point, I channeled my rage into attacking my larger foe and quickly struck him, knocking him down to the ground.

In an unexpected position of power, I demanded an apology for his behavior, and I got it.

In retrospect, this incident spoke to the accumulation of my childhood traumas. I felt an urge deep within me to protect others and to strike back at bullies. I completed my year at Veterans Memorial Junior High School, playing baseball in the spring. enjoying and benefiting from the skills instilled in me by my teachers and coaches.

From there I went onto Fitchburg High School. It was during this time that I became exposed to alcohol and found that drinking with friends gave me a sense of release that I never had before. I was able to let my guard down and have fun. I had several incidents of drinking too much, but for the most part I spent most time sober and dating a sweetheart in high school until I graduated.

Despite my growing addiction to alcohol, I made two promises to myself during my teenage years. First, I would never allow myself to impregnate a girl, and second, I would never use hard drugs. In my times of mass confusion and uncertainty, these were two issues that I would never compromise. After graduation, I enrolled in community college, but quickly dropped out. I preferred spending my time drinking and socializing rather than applying myself to my studies. My abuse of alcohol culminated in my arrest by the Fitchburg police.

I met a young woman from Long Island while vacationing with my friends on Cape Cod. We were married a year later, me at the ripe old age of nineteen. This teen marriage lasted less than three years and resulted in the birth of my only child. Despite having a short, immature marriage marred by alcohol, the gift of my daughter was the beginning of my journey back to sobriety and responsibility.

Sometime around the age of twenty-four and already divorced, I woke up one day and decided that I did not like the way my life was going. I was working two jobs to support my daughter and eventually stopped going out to socialize and began to think seriously about my future.

I was employed in a local factory at a dead-end job that offered no promise for the future. I became the union president at this factory to help me channel my anger, this time, into my workplace. One positive outcome of this work experience was that the company agreed to pay for a college course. At that time, Fisher Junior College had just opened a satellite program in Fitchburg at a closed catholic high school. I knew that starting an education was a beginning to better things in life.

School greatly reduced the time I spent drinking, but it wasn't until I began my first class in Business Math that reality slammed me in the face. Shortly after starting this basic course, I began doing homework that entailed adding up a large column of numbers. I soon realized that I could not concentrate well enough to add these digits and get to the final answer. I cried in shock and dismay at my inability to accomplish this elementary math problem and became deeply aware that I had to change my life.

Having hangovers in class was not helping my study habits and I knew that I did not like the way I felt physically. That discomfort was compounded by the fact that I was overweight and a heavy smoker. I decided it was time to change my ways. I stopped drinking immediately. A short while later, I quit smoking cold turkey and decided to take up running. I probably ran about 100 yards the first time out before I stopped, winded and gasping for air. Slowly but surely, it became easier to incorporate a routine of running and eating right.

After I was sober, I began to learn what effects alcohol abuse had inflicted on my life, and what my drinking was doing to me. It had stunted my ability to focus and to think clearly. As I got healthier, I got stronger. My newfound love of running helped me get into shape and I came to realize how much alcohol had cost me. I swore to myself I would never drink again.

The economic downturn of the mid-1970s resulted in being frequently laid off from my factory job. As luck would have it, a part time job opened up at a local alcohol detox center. I wanted to work there to help others, but I also had a strong desire to learn why I had abused alcohol. I worked there for over a year and received an intense education on alcohol abuse. I saw firsthand what alcohol does to a person, in terms of the destruction of life, both spiritually and physically. It also gave me the opportunity to work with people who needed my help.

In my sobriety, I realized that it was my calling to be of service to others, a goal that was consistent with my newfound desire to serve my community as a police officer. It felt as if a veil had been lifted. Emerging from the darkness of alcoholism afforded me a new lease on life.

With vigor, I began to focus on becoming a police officer. This entailed studying for and earning a passing score on the state civil service exam. My desire to be a police officer in my home city of Fitchburg never wavered despite failing to score high enough on the exam two years in a row. I hoped that the third time was a charm. I doubled down on my studying efforts. Familiar with the test structure, I was better prepared to excel. I was 25 years old, and my time was divided into working, studying, and raising my daughter.

I was elated to learn that my third effort on the civil service exam resulted in a score of 88, finally high enough to land my noble quest. Being single and divorced, I saw my chance to work as a police officer as a new beginning to support my child and create opportunities for her that I had only dreamed of in the past. It was a very satisfying feeling. Besides providing for my family and creating new financial opportunities, I would also be assuming a well-respected position of honor in my community.

The next step to reaching my goal of becoming a police officer was an appointment by the mayor. The names of those scoring highest on this civil service test were sent to the mayor's office. The mayor was given three names for every open position and by law was able to pick any one of three individuals from the list. Past practice dictated that candidates were selected in order of those who scored highest on the civil service test.

When I saw the list at City Hall, I was proud to see that I was number one for eligibility with my appointment occurring a few weeks later. Four proposed names were submitted to the City Council by the mayor for approval, and I found out that my name was not among them to be considered for appointment even though I was the top scoring candidate on the list. This news created a deep feeling of anxiety and fear. I had no idea why I was being unfairly bypassed by the mayor. Those feelings resulted in a hurried visit to City Hall. I had to find out why I was being excluded.

As I entered the mayor's office, the mayor's assistant was seated at his large brown desk in a swivel chair in front of me, a knowing look spread across his face. I immediately told him that I wanted to find out why I was not on the list to be appointed for the position of police officer. He told me that I was not being appointed because I currently lived in Westminster, a small town bordering Fitchburg. Living in Westminster over the last six months had no legal bearing on my appointment because civil service rules required that anyone taking the exam had to live in the city where they chose to work for one year prior to taking the exam. I had easily fulfilled this residency requirement as I had lived in Fitchburg my whole life. Knowing that this answer made no sense, I then asked to speak to the mayor directly. The mayor's assistant responded, "The mayor does not want to talk to you."

I was crushed by a feeling of helplessness at being so callously dismissed. After going through over a year's process from test taking to appointment time, I was having the door slammed in my face. This situation left me stunned, speechless and devastated. I left the mayor's office with my head down, in a state of confusion and anger, and went to visit my parents to inform them of this news.

Sitting in the kitchen at my parents' house, I lamented my predicament. I was feeling sorry for myself when my father, in his bombastic manner, said to me, "What's the matter with you? You have to fight this situation and make it right!"

He had this confrontational way about him from surviving World War II and being a professional boxer early in life. He knew the meaning of the word "fight."

His words shocked me out of my despair and set me thinking about what I could do to right this wrong. At this time, I was still working in a factory in Westminster and had become good friends with our fiery ex-union president named Dick O'Leary. Dick was a colorful and shrewd Irish labor representative who had led a successful strike at this factory in the past and knew how to go about fighting for justice. I told Dick about my dilemma.

Dick immediately reacted. "Eddy, you need to get a good Irish lawyer. I know just the guy for you. His name is Ed Ryan, and he has a practice in Fitchburg. Give him a call."

Returning home after work, I called Attorney Ed Ryan's office in Fitchburg and was able to speak to him directly. I told him my plight and asked if he could help.

Ed Ryan listened quietly to my story, then said, "Let me make a phone call and I will get back to you."

About twenty minutes after I hung up, he called back. I anxiously waited to hear what he had to say. He shocked me when he said, "You're all set. You're going to be appointed and you're going to the police academy!"

Sheer joy and elation percolated through my body as I hung up the phone. My dream was about to come true.

I was appointed a full-time police officer on October 22, 1980, along with three other candidates. It was then that I learned that Attorney Ed Ryan was the city solicitor, the chief legal advisor to the mayor. My fortune had changed dramatically, and I was about to embark on a lifelong journey that eventually lead to working as a police chief and an international police advisor in various locations around the world.

Only later did I realize that my status as a white male and city resident allowed me to access this attorney. I wondered how someone new to the community and someone of color would have been able to navigate the same challenges to get this job. How would it be possible for someone who does not have local contacts in the white community or understand the political power structure? I believe that had I been a person of color, I may never have become a police officer.

CHAPTER 3

Learning Policing: The Real Story

  The nearly two-hour ride from Fitchburg to Topsfield was not my idea of a pleasure drive but knowing that I was enrolled and attending the Police Academy gave me a sense of satisfaction. It was November of 1980, and every Monday morning, I was summoned outside my house by the honking of a behemoth four-door sedan.

  Relegated to the back seat behind my two classmates, I would ride to the academy and stay until Friday afternoon before returning home for the weekend. This was my routine for the next twenty weeks. Although my training would eventually cover a myriad of legal and policy studies, my education as a police officer actually began in the car on the way to the academy.

  In conversations with my colleagues, sandwiched in by the hilarity of the morning DJs on the radio, I began to learn about police culture. One of my roommates had a background in corrections and the other was a street-smart athlete who had attended college in Boston. Their life experiences were quite different from mine.

Growing up in Fitchburg, I had been taught to always see the best in others. I was quickly outflanked by my classmates who would remind me daily of how naive I was, especially to the world of policing. Whether we were chatting about a person or a topic, I would usually take a positive point of view. The guys were quick to remind me, in tag team style, that most people were dirt bags and wondered why on earth I would think otherwise.

One of their favorite responses to my idealistic nature was "Eddy! Wake up and smell the coffee!"

This was not the shining image of police work that I had imagined or expected. The opportunity to attend the academy and to serve on the police department in my hometown was a brand-new start for me. I felt that police work was so much more than a job, that instead, it was a calling, consistent with my upbringing and my desire to work in an honorable profession. I saw myself as the Irish kid fulfilling his destiny of becoming either a priest, a politician or a police officer, as the old saying went.

Memorizing the laws and learning the techniques of policing would prove less difficult than dealing with the police culture. Upon beginning classes at the academy, I was struck by the diversity of candidates from the different departments in attendance. One affable fellow was an undertaker who finally was realizing his dream to be a police officer. Another gentleman was a kindhearted soul from the State Environmental Police. There were likable candidates from every career background you could possibly imagine, and each person had the same goal in mind: to become an accredited police officer in the Commonwealth of Massachusetts.

It wasn't long before I learned there was also a dark side to some candidates coming to the job. A couple of classmates from the Boston area soon established themselves as the alpha males in the class, with one embracing the role of class bully. He was a carpenter from Southie, a predominantly Irish neighborhood in Boston. He was large in stature and bravado, routinely surveying our classes with a keen eye, assessing our strengths and weaknesses. If he did not like your opinion, he made it clear that he not only disagreed but wanted to humiliate you for it. Anyone who dared to challenge his authority was mocked and sent the unspoken message that you could be beaten for disagreeing with him.

As he took his usual spot in the back of the class, I could overhear his cocky voice talking about heading to the Elks Club to have a beer immediately after class. He was the first of many police officers that I would see struggle with substance abuse.

My time spent working with people in recovery, and being in recovery myself, made me acutely aware of the signs exhibited when individuals were in the grips of addiction. It did not matter whether they were genetically predisposed, if they grew up in an unstable home environment like my own, or if alcohol and drugs were a coping mechanism, addiction was rampant in this field of work. Even in these early days in the academy, I witnessed how booze could warp someone's mind.

I would see this insidious problem at all levels of my career. This was not the only familiar problem in police culture that would plague me for decades. Domestic violence proliferated police work, both in the field and in the department. I was shocked to learn, during a class on family disturbances, that a man who beat a woman in his home could not be arrested. That was a time before modern mandatory arrests laws were passed.

Our criminal laws were based on English Common law that professed that, "A man's home is his castle," and therefore, unless an officer saw the assault on his partner, there was nothing that could be done. Besides offering to take the abusive husband for a ride, the only policing strategy an officer could use was to engage in a bizarre form of couple's counseling, attempting to convince a typically intoxicated man to stop harming his spouse.

Upon hearing this particular piece of information, I was repulsed by what I interpreted to be a legal justification for spousal abuse and domestic violence. It was unfathomable to me that human suffering could be unquestioned and ostensibly ignored by law enforcement. I could not stomach the notion of enforcing a law that protected a violent offender and allowed for repeated brutality.

I felt my hand raise to get the instructor's attention, then said that this did not make sense. Before the words were out of my mouth I was told to "shut up" by the classroom bully. Looking around the room I became aware that many of my colleagues in policing chose not to question the law but instead to blindly follow it. To speak up about injustice was naive and put a bull's eye on my back.

I witnessed an example of the glaring injustice of this law about a year after graduating from the academy. I was sent to a family disturbance call in South Fitchburg on Thanksgiving night. My partner and I were let into the apartment by a crying woman. She was clearly in distress, leaning against a wall, holding a blood-soaked towel to her head. The woman reported that she had been assaulted, thrown across the room by her husband. She struck her head on an iron radiator resulting in a bloody, matted gash. Hysterically crying, the woman tried to explain through her heaving sobs that her husband was just released from prison on parole, and that he had gotten drunk and beat her. The raging husband staggered into the room, bellowing "This is my house! This is none of your business! Get the fuck out!"

According to the laws on the books in 1981, the husband was right. I called for an ambulance to provide medical attention to the wife's gaping wound and eventually called the assailant's parole officer. But my hands were tied. There was nothing more I could do to protect the woman, and I had no recourse against this brutal man because he was in his own home. I quietly cleared the scene, leaving this raving lunatic in charge of this marriage.

Many of my academy classmates would accept this kind of behavior without question. But acceptance of these injustices and negative attitudes towards human behavior were not ubiquitous. I found myself gravitating towards likeminded people of integrity who embodied the more noble principles of police work. I have heard it said that people look for themselves in others and believe this to be true. I made friends with several colleagues who shared my minority point of view in this mostly male, macho culture. In fact, a couple of my friends were maybe a little too open.

One night, a couple of classmates invited me to smoke a joint with them. I was not surprised but politely turned them down. I thought it would be hypocritical for me to smoke marijuana knowing that I would soon have to arrest people for the same thing in the future. This did not seem consistent with the type of police officer I wanted to be. It was becoming more apparent that I did not fit in with the mainstream cop culture of the time. I could neither blindly follow the law, like my colleagues who accepted antiquated laws condoning domestic violence. In the same vein, I would not blatantly ignore the law and engage in recreational drug use.

When I did not openly condemn my two pot smoking colleagues or shun them, the attitude of some was that I was not true cop material. I began to be openly victimized by cop culture because I thought for myself and did not carry the common views of my classmates. One person at the academy suggested that I was in the wrong profession and called me "a liberal social worker."

I was not just attacked verbally for my divergent viewpoints. When it came time for learning hand-to-hand combat and tactical takedown strategies, I became the physical whipping boy for those who did not like my opinions. Despite being in the best physical condition of my life, thanks to running and a diet free from alcohol and drugs, I did not possess much upper body strength.

It was my classmate from Southie, the bulky carpenter and his sidekick friend who had the assigned task of arresting me, a part of class work. The two were charged with taking me down and handcuffing me while I resisted their arrest. I tried with every ounce of strength I had to withstand them, but I was quickly overpowered and slammed to the floor. Their message was clear: they hated me, and this was my punishment. I accepted this treatment and sensed from some people that I had it coming.

Being different from the perceived stereotype of a cop was not valued at the academy, and I was seeing this firsthand. Here I was, a white Irish guy being hassled for having less than popular beliefs. And I knew I was not the only one suffering for it. We had one Black officer in the class who also happened to be a woman. She had come from a state agency, and she spent her academy time in complete isolation. Instead of staying at the Academy Monday through Friday like many of the men did, she commuted daily. This was a time when women were not totally accepted in policing and as it turned out, if you were a woman of color, you had even more obstacles to overcome. She struggled at times to perform the physical requirements of the job, and this did not pass unnoticed by some of my classmates.

I remember one incident where she was running, and two guys felt she was not going fast enough or putting in the effort. One of them yelled in her direction, "Put a stolen hubcap under her arm and watch how fast she can run then!"

Having acknowledged my own biases and prejudices, it wasn't long before I saw that feelings of racism were alive and present in policing. In retrospect, I knew this commentary about the Black candidate was wrong, but at the time I did not have the courage to speak up. I am ashamed to admit that I even went along with the "joke" and laughed. How that woman ever made it through the academy I will never know.

In retrospect, I think I had a harder time navigating the more informal, unspoken aspects of the academy. While memorizing laws and learning policy was challenging, I had a single-minded focus on being academically successful. We were required to pass several exams, and I had committed myself to studying hard and getting good grades from early on. I accomplished this and was able to close out my studies in a fairly relaxed atmosphere. Some of my classmates, on the other hand, had not made learning a priority and struggled mightily to pass the final exams. We also had physical graduation requirements in addition to our academic obligations. One last highlight of my physical training was placing first in the mile for my class. But I did not finish alone. I chose to run my qualifying mile in a tie finish with my friend from the Environmental Police.

The class bully chimed in sarcastically, "Way to go. You're probably going to be chief someday."

Our days at the academy were over and it was now time to begin our careers back in our respective departments. My first day on the job, I reported to the office of the shift commander for roll call. I arrived early, ahead of the other officers who were starting the 3-11pm shift with me. The officer in charge was sitting at his desk going through his drawers when he looked up at me and shouted, "Who the fuck are you?"

While my commander's response was obviously a form of hazing, it was also my initiation. That was my official introduction to policing in Fitchburg.

Taking to the streets as a rookie was a hit or miss experience. Modern day field training for police officers was not yet in existence, so in the 1980s you learned the ropes of how to be a police officer by making mistakes. Today, when a police officer graduates from the academy, they are assigned to a specially trained field officer responsible for monitoring and mentoring a new officer who begins working on the street. The new officer is constantly evaluated over a period of time, and if the training officer believes the candidate has reached a high enough level of competency, then the probationary period is concluded. The officer is then allowed to work on their own.

  Initially, I was assigned to work with an officer, Jim Raymond, who did things by the book, and I gratefully learned from him. He was especially good as he took on the role of a helper. He encouraged questions and provided direct answers. Jim lent his experience to me in the best way he could. Soon thereafter, I was put on the 6pm to 2am shift. Two of us were assigned to this shift that overlapped the 3-11pm and the 11pm to 7am shift. We were supposed to be reinforcements during these peak hours of activity. I was assigned to work with another fairly new officer, and we rode together in the same cruiser. I quickly learned two things. First, we were put together because the older officers wanted no part of having to train us. Second, the old timers actually liked the fact that we were new because we would take their calls, making their shift easier.

  One of the calls that we took on a Saturday night still stands out in my mind. The officer and I were on patrol when we received a dispatch to find a payphone. This was in the days before cell phones, and we had to call into the department. This usually meant something sensitive was going on and they did not want to broadcast the information out to people listening to their police scanners.

Navigating lower Main Street, we quickly found a phone, dropping in a dime to reach the station. The officer on the desk picked up the phone and gave us our orders. We needed to head to Charlie's Bar on North Street, an establishment primarily patronized by Black people who did not appreciate white police officers.

We received further instructions that there were two real tall Black guys in the bar having an argument. One of the guys is wearing a tuxedo and he has a gun on him. The caller was afraid something is going to happen.

I answered "OK," but the immediate thought echoing in my brain was that it sounded dangerous and that someone should really call the police. Then it sank in. This is what I had signed up for and it was up to me to go in to take the gun away.

I hung up the phone receiver and returned to the police cruiser. I immediately told my partner what was going on and we embarked on our short ride over to the bar. We pulled up to the front of the bar to an overflow crowd on the sidewalk. It was busy for a hot summer night, and I could hear the blast of music from the jukebox inside.

Our appearance immediately drew surprised and resentful eyes toward us as we got out of the vehicle. Opening the door, we were met with the sound of loud voices mingling with the music and a constant stare from the patrons who telegraphed the question, "What the hell are you doing here?" It was almost like the scene from "Animal House" when the white college students went into a Black bar and saw their favorite Black singer, Otis, who they hired for frat parties. They shouted out, "Otis, my man!" and received a cold stare from Otis who acted like he had never seen them before.

It was time to get down to business. To my immediate right stood two tall Black men arguing face to face in a heated manner. I instinctively walked into the small place between them. As I stood in the middle, I could hear their raised threatening voices toward each other. I looked up at the guy in the tuxedo and said "I got a call that you have a gun on you. Is that true?"

He gave me a look to acknowledge that he heard my question, but never said a word in response. He went right on arguing with the other man. Announcing my intentions, I told him that I was going to pat him down to make sure he did not have a weapon. I used the calmest manner that I could muster, thanking God that no one in the bar could see my knees knocking against each other. Upon performing a short, cursory pat down of his outer body, I was unable to locate a weapon of any kind. I told him that I was all set and walked away with my partner, stepping back outside to the heat and humidity of the July night.

I quickly noticed a backup unit with two veteran officers seated in the police car and announced to the fellow cops that no weapon had been found and we cleared the scene. I never admitted it, but this was the first time on the job that I was scared shitless.

Eventually, I ended up walking a beat in the Latino section of the city. The neighborhood was in transition from an old Italian neighborhood to a new wave of Latino immigrants taking up residence. There was a still-functioning Italian family market that made the best sausages in the world operated by a World War II vet and his sweet, street-smart wife. He still suffered from his service injuries. They were part of the greatest generation and had eked out a living running this store for many years.

Across the street was the hangout dominated by Latino teens who would play music, make noise like kids do, and at times sell drugs. The Italian market had a birds' eye view of the activity, and the owners would often call the station when it looked as though something was going down. On several occasions, I was able to use stealth methods to catch a drug deal in real time. Forsaking my uniform, I would camouflage in plain street clothes to make a bust. Other days, I could time it so that I would drive around a corner down the wrong way on a one-way street in order to be right on top of the dealers before they could react.

On one occasion, I pulled up and a kid was right in the middle of showing his wares to the driver of a stopped car who was handing over his money. I got out of my cruiser, chased the guy dealing drugs, and collared him for the arrest. On many a night, this scene would play itself out.

The teens on the street had taken to calling me "The Harasser" because I was constantly checking on them. I didn't like the name, but I felt somewhat vindicated when the head of the detective bureau defended me one night. When a fellow cop had mentioned that the neighborhood kids called me "The Harasser," my superior said, "The kids don't like him because he's doing his job."

My continuing success in interrupting drug dealing on the street did not go unnoticed. I felt my stock rise among my fellow officers. No longer did I have to endure the "white, liberal social worker" talk from my colleagues; now, just silent respect and a little bit of envy for what I was doing.

It wasn't until one night that I made my bones on the street that my reputation as a solid cop took hold for good. It was a late fall evening, and I was assigned to South Fitchburg. I was solo that night, working alone in my cruiser, when I received a call that a woman had just reported that she had been robbed at Rose's Department Store. I switched on my blue lights and drove to the store as fast and as safely as I could.

Pulling into the parking lot, I was met by a young woman in her early twenties who was shaking and visibly upset. She told me that when she came out of the store, a man came up from behind her and put a gun to her head. She heard him cock the hammer on the pistol as he demanded her money and she immediately complied. The robber took her money and fled the area on foot.

I began to check the area with the other officers on scene, looking for the suspect. When I asked for a description of the thief, the victim reported that he was masked and that she never saw his face but described him as young and stocky. Still new to my job, I was taken aback by how shaken up this young woman was, and she grew angrier as time went on. After searching for some time, the police cars cleared the scene when they were unable to locate the robber.

Thinking on my feet, I invited the victim to get in the front seat of the cruiser with me to case the area. I always felt it was a good idea to cruise the area after the activity ceased on the off chance that the person who committed the crime was hiding or laying low. After several minutes of slowly driving through the adjoining neighborhood, I saw a person emerge from a wooded area on the poorly lit street. The young lady immediately said that it could be the suspect we were looking for. I informed the young woman that I was going to approach the man and told her that if something happened, she should use the radio to call the station.

Understanding that the victim had not seen the robber's face, I knew I had to approach this man slowly and cautiously. I stopped the car and got out, calling for the man to stop. I asked him what he was doing there, and he responded by saying that he was going home. Looking for a weapon, I reached forward with my right arm to pat down the front waistline of his pants, and he immediately pushed me away. Certain that I had the right guy, I lunged for him, and a wrestling match ensued.

I did not know it at the time but the lady in my cruiser had done what I suggested and had radioed the station to report what she saw. Before long, a fellow officer showed up on the scene. I saw him getting out of his car yelling "Hang on, Eddy!" as he came to my aid.

We wrestled the guy to the ground. When we had control of the robber, I began to search him and yelled, "Where is the gun?"

"In my pants," he said.

Reaching deep into the waistline of his pants, I pulled out a blue steeled .357 loaded handgun. Since the struggle was ongoing, I tossed it away from all three of us. With the help of my savior backup, Phil Kearns, we proceeded to cuff the robber and brought him over to the cruiser. Before we could lower him into the back of the car, the woman flew out of the front seat, screaming in anger at the assailant for what he had done to her earlier. I transported him to the police station where my captain, the shift commander who had first greeted me when I started on the job, booked the prisoner. A man of few words, he didn't say much to me, but he was beaming with pride at the arrest I made.

After the robber was placed in a cell, I went up to the detective bureau on the second floor of the police department. It was kind of hallowed ground for uniformed officers as they never spend much time there. I was greeted at the door of the bureau by the savvy, experienced night detective, Kevin O'Brien, who held the blue gun in his hand. Looking down at it, he said to me, "Nice grab, Eddy."

This was an unofficial announcement that I had earned his respect.

If this incident was not enough confirmation that I was accepted and had arrived as a police officer, fate had more in store for me. A short while before I nabbed this guy, the chief had instituted a commendation program that consisted of awarding medals. My captain was so impressed with my work that he wrote me up for the Commendation for Bravery on the night of this incident. A couple of days later, I was at roll call for my 3-11pm shift when the chief made an unusual appearance. He read out a commendation for me and the other officer who assisted in the arrest.

I received the first Red Commendation Badge for Bravery ever bestowed upon a Fitchburg police officer. The chief left the roll call and I picked up the letter and the attached commendation pin. I had no idea what to do with it. It was then that my streetwise sergeant, John O'Leary, removed the pin from the attached paper and affixed it on my chest just above my badge. I had arrived.

CHAPTER 4

UMASS Lowell: Putting in the Extra Effort

After overcoming the skepticism that some members of the department held about me, I felt that I finally earned their respect. Despite being different, there was no longer any question that I was not only capable of doing the job as a police officer, but that I could perhaps even excel at it.

I found myself gravitating towards and building comradeships with the officers who had managed to master both the social and investigative roles of police work. These colleagues were relentless in their efforts to know their city and to never pass on unfinished work to the detective bureau. The officers that I respected and looked up to took great pride and satisfaction in solving their own problems and meeting challenges head on. They were not the kind of officer who avoided work, collected a paycheck, and got lost in the world of civil service unaccountability, or as my mentor called it, "retiring the day they started."

A key distinguishing factor I noticed was that good police officers felt a sense of responsibility to the neighborhoods they worked. I made it a point to know all of the people I served, both citizens and criminals. When someone was disrupting a neighborhood by breaking into houses, it was our duty to stop this behavior, to hold the person accountable, and to comfort those who had been violated and victimized. This was not a job for us, but rather a vocation.

Working in this kind of environment felt fulfilling. I learned from my fellow officers who were constantly evaluating their own job performance. We grew to promote a healthy competition and prided ourselves on creativity in performing our duties. Whether it was solving local house breaks, car thefts, or armed robbery, we all felt responsible to do our best work to solve our cases.

One common theme that I learned was the old police adage, "You'll get a lot more done using honey than vinegar." It proved true, time and time again, that being nice to people, especially criminals, would yield better results than being mean. There was a time to show authority, but more important was having the humility and humanity to relate to people's circumstances. While the academy taught me how to do police work by the book, I was learning from my colleagues that one could bring innovation and creativity to the job. Often these qualities also carried over into the personal lives of my fellow officers.

One of the most creative and best police officers I ever worked with was Joel Kaddy. He taught me that learning how to talk to people and get them to tell you what you wanted to know was an art form that was cultivated by creating trust with not only the community but even, as Joel pointed out, the worst of the bad guys.

Joel worked for many years as a uniformed police officer in a very close-knit neighborhood called Cleghorn. He quickly realized that if you did not get along with people you would not be able to do your job. No one would talk to you. Cleghorn was an area where a multitude of crimes took place, from breaking and entering into buildings to the most serious assaults, including murder.

As happens with most police work, law enforcement involvement usually begins after the crime has occurred. The physical presence of the police is not much of a preventive measure in suppressing crime.

There are only so many ways to solve crime. Many times, it is contingent on witnesses to the crime coming forward and being willing to testify in court. Sometimes people hear information about who committed a crime and they tell, resulting in a responding officer making an arrest and interrogation, hopefully resulting in a confession and a conviction in court.

But it wasn't until Joel related a story about a series of armed robberies that were taking place in Cleghorn that one could fully appreciate his efforts. One convenience store robbery yielded a video of the crime. The video was taken to the police station and viewed by several officers. Although the video did not clearly identify the robber, Joel guessed it was a certain individual that he was familiar with in the neighborhood where he worked. One of the other officers thought it might be that individual's brother, but Joel was certain, as he recognized the distinctive gait of this individual.

He decided to take the video to the suspect's apartment in Cleghorn and show it to his mother. The mother was a matriarch of the neighborhood who knew that her sons were sometimes not on the right side of the law. In this case Officer Kaddy knew the mother, and he knew that she and all mothers he encountered did not want their kids "to grow up to be cowboys"— meaning, dangerous criminals. He plugged in a VCR he brought with him, loaded the tape and showed it to the mother. The mother immediately identified the son that Joel had identified and said, "That's my boy!"

Joel asked the mother to get her son to turn himself in to the police. He promised her that no one would hurt him, and he would be treated fairly. Both he and the mother knew that this had to stop before her son or someone else was killed or badly injured. The mother convinced her son to turn himself in, ending the crime wave and more importantly, doing so without anyone getting hurt.

Joel went onto tell me that he developed a friendly relationship with the mother over the years. He told me, with a glint in his eye and a musing smile, that he used to go to the mother's house after his 3-11 pm shift and bring her a six-pack of Narraganset beer along with tomato juice, and they would have a nightcap together called a Red Eye.

This story was so revealing of Joel's nature; he was ahead of his time and understanding of police work that is not common today. The mother and son were black and poor, but Joel looked beyond all this cultural difference, especially during those times, and saw a mother who was struggling with poverty. This woman was no different than any other parent in her love and hope for her children. Joel's modeling of building relationships had a profound effect on me at the time and even more in the future when I became a police chief.

While policing, with all of its duties and obligations, was indeed a full-time vocation, for some this work alone was not enough. I noticed how several cops used their energy and wits to create different ventures outside of their shifts and their details. Some officers put in all kinds of extra effort to build successful businesses in their off-duty time. Others built beautiful properties. As for me, I was never blessed with the attributes of entrepreneurship or trade skills. I sensed that I needed to put in the extra effort to be more successful in life and I decided to do this by continuing my education. I came to the job with an associate degree in business management. It was an accomplishment I was proud of, but I soon learned that advancing my education while on the job could be quite lucrative.

Massachusetts and the city of Fitchburg had adopted a career incentive program law that came about after the police campus protests and riots in the 1960s. Born from a piece of legislation called the Quinn Bill, this police education initiative was named after the state representative who sponsored it. The program provided cash incentives for police to obtain a degree in criminal justice with the eventual goal of increasing police professionalism and performance through higher education. A secondary, yet equally important goal of providing police with a post-secondary education, was to instill a better understanding of and relationship with college students during the turbulent times when it first went into effect.

When I enrolled as a part-time student, the incentives were incremental increases in pay depending upon the degree you earned: a 10% salary increase for obtaining an associate degree, a 20% increase for a bachelor's degree, and a 25% increase for a master's degree. Having already obtained my associate degree, I only had to complete one year of studies, consisting of all the criminal justice courses to get an associate degree in criminal justice.

I enrolled at Mount Wachusett Community College in Gardner, Massachusetts. The eventual increase in salary was appreciated, but it soon became apparent that the courses that I took were lacking in relevance, and in some cases were just a waste of time. To be clear, courses like Psychology and The History of Minority Groups were excellent and were taught by seasoned academics, but the criminal justice courses were new, and there was a serious lack of content being taught by practitioners.

Despite these issues, I was determined to keep moving forward. One of the unforeseen outcomes of my attending the Mount was meeting a woman at lunch one day. Her name was Sue, and she was divorced with two children. Our connection was immediately strong, and we entered into a new relationship and eventually marriage. Sue added a sense of security and support to my endeavors.

Stepping into this role also meant establishing a new balance between my personal life, my professional responsibilities, and academic endeavors. Being a conscientious police officer required an extended effort beyond a typical 40-hour week. Countless hours spent in court waiting to give testimony and working extra details often resulted in a minimum of a 60-hour work week. Although it would have been easier to enroll in a college closer to home, I was determined to get an education that would serve me well.

I realized early on that many of my fellow officers in my department and throughout the state attended collegiate programs that were "designed" for police officers. Certain academic institutions chose to exploit the revenues taken in by these programs by supporting diploma mills. In many instances, poorly qualified instructors gave out passing grades to absentee students that ultimately resulted in a statewide scandal of fraud and cheating. I often referred to these college programs sarcastically as "Wossamatta U" education. I was determined that when I continued my academic learning, I would steer clear of those kinds of programs.

After considering my local options for a bachelor's degree program, I decided to transfer to the University of Lowell in Lowell, Massachusetts. Beginning this program was quite a challenge. It required a 60-mile round trip commute every time I attended class. My schedule usually consisted of going to classes at least three days a week, plus off-hour and weekend visits to the university library.

The internet was not yet accessible to a college student like me in 1986, so I did research by scouring library catalogues and then locating those books and periodicals for information. Taking on this responsibility along with my job obligations amounted to a commitment of more than 75 hours every week.

I was impressed with the quality of education that I received at the University of Lowell. My professors were nationally acclaimed for their research and experience. The Introduction to Criminal Justice textbook used in my program was the gold standard all over the country and was penned by one of my professors at the time. Another professor was a nationally recognized teacher and researcher in the field of statistics and quantitative methods. A few years after graduating from Lowell, I attended a presentation to an international group of police officers at the FBI National Academy in Quantico, Virginia. While there, I was pleasantly surprised to see that one of my professors was cited in a national study on missing children that was presented to this group.

Lastly, and most fondly, I was proud of my association with Dr. Eve Buzawa, who was a nationally recognized expert on the subject of domestic violence and police response. Her classes and research interests had a major impact on me. During the mid-1980s, policing finally began to accept and incorporate research from academia into field work and training.

A game changer in police work was the publication of the Minnesota Domestic Violence Police Response Study that examined a variety of effective responses to ending domestic violence. It measured and compared police responses like counseling at these calls versus making arrests. The study showed that arresting was the most effective response as it ended the domestic violence incident immediately and had a deterrent effect. The study also found that this response was not perfect in holding offenders accountable.

Studies like these broke some long-standing stereotypes, namely ending the common standard that "a man's home is his castle," affirming for me my gut reaction to domestic violence at the police academy. Academic research proved to me and my colleagues that holding violent offenders accountable was the right way to approach domestic violence.

Learning at the University of Lowell not only exposed me to the best of research and knowledge in the field of criminal justice, but it also opened many other doors for me. While working on a term paper, I needed to locate government research documents that were not available at my campus library. Fortunately, I found the materials that I needed were located in the library of Wellesley College in Wellesley, Massachusetts, a prestigious, all female liberal arts college. I drove to the college on a weekday when I was not working.

I vividly remember driving on a beautiful fall day accented by a rich foliage of red, green, and yellow leaves as I pulled into the parking lot of their library. I got out of my car and immediately noticed a pristine, stone gothic building that appeared to be the campus chapel straight ahead. Alongside the chapel was the library building. Unlike the University of Lowell, which was always brimming with students rushing in and out, the atmosphere was almost serene, with motion at a much slower pace as students moved leisurely in and out of the building.

Entering through the front doors, I found myself in a lobby filled with comfortable couches and hardwood tables. As I was taking in this new setting, a woman of stately bearing approached me and said, "How do you do? Can I help you, sir?" in the most pleasant and professional voice.

Her greeting lent an air of dignity to my person, and I felt her sincere desire to assist me. I informed the librarian of my research project and had written down a list of documents that I needed. She asked to see my list, and I handed it over to her. Requesting that I follow her, she led me to a beautiful oak desk and chair, where she invited me to take a seat. She took leave, and returned several minutes later, having located all the documents that I was looking for. The research librarian had even gone above and beyond, bringing me other research materials that she thought would be helpful. She then put one of the books in front of me, opened it, creased the book and said, "I think you will find this book quite helpful in your research."

    I ended up writing the best research paper of my academic career. I knew in my heart that these labors in my education were bound to bear fruit. I opted against the programs specially designed for police officers, the rubber stamp programs, the diploma mills that handed out degrees for cops with spotty attendance and poor academic performance. I refused to take the path of least resistance. I wanted a degree that I would be proud to attain, and I got that at the University of Lowell, where I received what would turn out to be a life changing education.

Chapter 5

Learning the Job: Trying to Organize Chaos

Since my start with the Fitchburg Police Department in the spring of 1981, I had worked as a patrol officer for nine years before being promoted to sergeant in 1990. During those years, working the streets of a small urban city, I had a front row seat to some of the best and worst that humanity had to offer. Fitchburg had a proud history but was now an economically depressed community with changing demographics, ranging from racial make-up to a rising crime rate.

I suppose that my experience during this time was not much different than a lot of my colleagues. What became painfully obvious to me was the realization that the events requiring my response were often rooted in measures well beyond my control. Police officers working the streets of Fitchburg in the early 1980s were at a distinct disadvantage that we had no idea existed.

During this time, the city had a mayor who did not support the police chief. This was reflected in how poorly staffed we were as a department. In a city of 45,000 people, it was not unusual to see only three police officers deployed during a shift. As officers, we accepted the fact that we were consistently short-handed. This reality exploded upon me when one summer Sunday morning I was dispatched to a call of a man shooting a gun at his wife. With no one else to take the call, I arrived at the scene alone.

I was charged with making the snap decision of whether I should wait for a backup or enter the house by myself to see if I could stop the situation or render aid as needed. I decided to enter the second floor of the apartment building. Running up the stairs, I passed two people on the stairway who were clearly upset and who pointed me to the apartment door where the trouble was. I opened the door, scanning the room for a weapon or a person holding a weapon, and saw neither. But I did immediately see a woman lying prone on the floor, bleeding profusely from her back.

I knelt down to take her pulse on her neck and could not find one. Referring to my medical training, I decided to perform CPR on the victim and tilted her head back to open her airway. Putting my mouth to hers, I exhaled a large breath into her body. To my shock and devastation, I heard a large gasp of air coming out of her back. In all my training in first aid and CPR, I had never learned about this kind of reaction while giving rescue breathing to a victim.

Stunned, I pulled away from her mouth and became aware that two first responders from the ambulance had arrived and were standing over me. They read the helpless expression on my face as I looked up at them. One of them stared at me, shaking his head, and said "She's gone."

I stood up and backed away as the medical people took over the scene. I tried to make sense of what had just happened. Residents standing on the porch of the apartment announced that the man who shot her had left before I had arrived. I put out a description of the suspect we were looking for when another police officer arrived on the scene. I guess I must have been a mess because the first thing he asked me was "Are you ok?"

I was somewhat dazed, but had the presence of mind enough to lie, shaking my head in the affirmative. Before we could begin to explain what had just taken place, dispatch was instructing me to clear the scene to handle another emergency. The dispatcher gave me the address of another home on my route. An upset man had locked himself in a room with a gun and was threatening to kill himself.

Snapping into action, I robotically assumed responsibility for this call, running back down the stairs to get into my police car. At the same time, the officer who had arrived on the scene to provide me with backup was also dispatched elsewhere, underscoring just how short staffed we were.

I was in my cruiser for less than five minutes before I pulled up to a stately, older single-family home. This was not the average house I frequented during a shift in this struggling and hurting city. I got out of my car and went to the side door of the home where a middle-aged woman and her daughter met me at the door. Both were highly alarmed and clearly frightened. I asked what was going on and the woman explained that her husband was in a room by himself with a gun and was threatening to hurt himself. Once again, I had been asked to singly handle a situation that was not the type of call for a young police officer to be handling on his own.

The woman pointed at a closed door off the living room and indicated that her husband was in there. I walked to the door and knocked. In as calm a manner I could muster in the moment, I announced my presence as a police officer, and I asked him if he was okay. Frankly, I don't remember exactly what he said, but I do remember that he did not want to talk with me or to cooperate with any of my requests.

Standing at the door alone, I felt a heightened sense of urgency to do something. Help was not coming. This was my problem, and my problem alone to solve. Perhaps I had been still reeling from the previous call where I was helpless and unable to save a life. But I knew I had to take action here to prevent a second tragedy.

In an instant, I grabbed the doorknob, turned it, and entered the room to see a middle-aged white man with a revolver in his hand. Without saying anything, I calmly walked over to him and reached for the gun, taking it away from him. He was openly distraught and crying. In the blink of an eye, the situation changed from a dangerous and potentially deadly encounter to one of nothing but compassion for this torn and wounded family. I reached for my radio and asked dispatch to send an ambulance. They arrived quickly and took the man to the emergency room for mental health treatment. I cleared the scene.

A short time later, I heard that the man who had fatally shot the woman earlier had been captured. He had been walking on the street not far from his house and was apprehended. Officers had also been able to locate the shotgun he had used in the killing. All of this had occurred in a less than an hour.

These experiences were all too common during my early days and happened far too frequently to ever forget. Working on a Labor Day weekend, the department was once again short-handed as we attempted to respond to a flurry of calls. There was no doubt that more officers should have been on the street, and we were feeling let down by our city, forced to make do with what we had on a very busy holiday weekend.

While driving my assigned route, I received a call to respond to a domestic dispute between a man and a woman. I drove up the steep hill to this neighborhood and came to a stop in front of a tenement building in a poor section of the city. I could see a pregnant woman and a man arguing outside in the yard. The woman yelled to me as I walked towards them that he had hit her. The Black man, who stood about 6 feet 5 inches tall, and weighed well over 225 pounds, yelled at me to get away. The danger of this domestic situation was imminent, and fortunately, another officer showed up to assist me.

Examining the circumstances of the situation, and considering the recently passed mandatory arrest law, my fellow officer and I realized that we needed to bring this man into the station for domestic assault and battery. He was agitated and refused to comply with our demands to submit to arrest. He, instead, assumed an uncooperative and defiant stance. Aware of the violent acts he was accused of and because of the large size of the man, I called for additional assistance on my portable radio. The radios we had been given were old and worn out, and to my dismay, my request for additional assistance was heard by others only as a garbled, indiscernible sound.

I approached the combative man and attempted to handcuff his wrist. He began to fight with me and my fellow officer. Soon, we found ourselves wrestling with the man on the ground, when I felt hands pulling on my back. I looked up and was astonished to see that the wife was trying to stop me from arresting him. I instinctively pushed her away and she fell to the ground. I pulled back from the suspect and removed my service baton from my duty belt. Without thinking, I deferred to my training, opting to use escalated force to arrest this man. I swung my baton at his knees and struck them squarely and firmly. I was surprised to see that employing this tactic was completely useless as he just stared at me. The scene was almost cartoon-like in nature, as I watched the baton absorb the blow and bend as it came in contact with the man's kneecaps.

The next thing I knew, the husband was in a fit of rage, grabbing and pulling at me. He managed to tear my uniform shirt off of my body. I again reached for my radio and called for help in a high pitch voice, but to no avail. The radio did not work. We continued to fight with the suspect until more help finally arrived, and we were able to subdue him and take him into custody. I subsequently wrote a report stating that the shorthanded situation, the lack of an operable radio system, and literally having my shirt torn off my back was humiliating and a disgrace to the department.

The report had an impact as this incident resulted in the department obtaining a new set of modern radios. I was also visited by a local councilman who came to my house to talk with me about the incident and to inquire about my well-being. Working with scarce resources and minimal support were only some of the challenges police officers faced in the mid-1980s.

My time at the University of Lowell was teaching me that solid research and good data could help identify patterns and explain certain behaviors. It became even more apparent to me that the proliferation of gun ownership in the United States clearly translated into more gun-related violent crime. America's fascination with and glorification of gun ownership is something I have never personally understood. Even working in law enforcement for the better part of my life, I have never enjoyed carrying or discharging a gun. Instead, I viewed my service weapon as a tool, a necessary evil, and approached all my calls praying they did not require me to use lethal force.

Although much of the public may assume that police are fervent gun enthusiasts, that assumption is far from the truth. I have never met a police officer who hasn't been asked the popular party question, "If I am in my house and someone breaks in, can I shoot him?"

Usually, this question originates from a gun aficionado inquiring about when it would be legal to shoot someone in self-defense. This question always bothered me to the point of ridiculousness, especially because I had seen first-hand the damaging effects and misuse of firearms in my own community. It was not unusual for me to be called in to investigate a shooting in the city.

On one particular afternoon, I was dispatched to a call of a man shot while entering a home. But the details of this case were certainly out of the ordinary. It turned out that a man was shot while he allegedly attempted to force entry into a house. Taken at face value, this seemed to be a rare occasion of an intruder being shot by a homeowner protecting himself and his property. The only problem was that there was a whole lot more to this story.

As it turned out, the homeowner was a gambler who had gotten in over his head. The home intruder was his bookie who had come to collect on the homeowner's gambling debt which he could not afford to pay. For too long, the homeowner had ignored the bookmaker, resulting in the visit to his home. At this point, the story gets hazy, as the homeowner claimed that the bookie forced his way into his house. Hearing a commotion, he grabbed his gun and shot the bookie in the leg at the bottom of the stairs, sustaining a non-life-threatening injury.

After taking statements from both parties involved, I was not surprised to see that the stories contradicted one another. The bookie claimed that the owner had invited him to come over to get his money. The intruder did not have a weapon, and he said the shooter told him by phone to come into the house. There was no forced entry at the scene. The homeowner claimed that, upon seeing the intruder, he feared for his life and shot the bookie.

Being familiar with the dishonest nature and the past crimes of the homeowner, the statements given, and the totality of the circumstances, I placed the homeowner under arrest for attempted murder among other charges. The case eventually went to trial. The defendant got an excellent lawyer who was able to convince a jury that the homeowner was protecting himself and was justified with shooting the intruder. I was and will always be convinced that this incident was simply a way for the shooter to escape his agreement to pay his debts and craftily composed a Second Amendment scenario to justify his evil intent. This was not only a perversion of the truth, but it was also a circumstance of someone twisting a law designed to protect people into the ultimate fantasy of a sick gun enthusiast.

The intent of the Second Amendment to bear arms and form a well-regulated militia was not meant to be a disguise to get away with murder. These incidents all reflect the wide range of profession-related challenges that I faced throughout my career. Whether it was dealing with the unintended consequences of an underfunded police department or contending with guilty individuals literally getting away with murder, this took a toll on me and other good cops in many ways. Moreover, I was not insulated from this pain on a personal level. While it had been my police report referencing broken radios that caught the attention of city politicians, I also earned some unwanted attention and notoriety when my own father was arrested.

As a World War II prisoner of war suffering from undiagnosed post-traumatic stress disorder, my father was known to act out from time to time. He would engage in altercations with his neighbors, and even the local kids who he perceived were infringing upon his property. He lived with my mother in a newly constructed small ranch that he was able to purchase brand new because of his status as a disabled veteran.

One of the first things he did after moving into the house was to erect a steel chain link fence around the property in a new neighborhood where there were no other fences. I understood the fence building to be symbolic of his experience as a prisoner of war enclosed in the confines of camp. In a sense, he was now the guard of the camp. Anytime he perceived neighborhood kids even setting foot near his fence, he would come out of the house yelling at them. It did not take long before the kids resorted to throwing stones at the house. Eventually, my father began meticulously collecting the rocks from his yard in order to volley them back at the neighborhood kids as they taunted each other from opposite sides of the partition.

On occasion, my fellow officers would approach me while on the job. They would question me, "How can you let this happen?" and tell me, "You have to stop this!"

Much like my life was during my childhood, I was powerless over my father. Nothing I had ever said had stopped him from performing his will, and my being a cop in the city where he lived was no deterrent. Despite talking with my mother and pleading with my father to change his ways, my requests fell on deaf ears.

Eventually, my father went too far. One of my fellow officers went to court and got a civil apprehension warrant to take my father before a judge and to have him medically and psychologically evaluated. The order was served while I was working, and my father was arrested and taken into custody after fighting with the officers and resisting arrest. He was brought into the station while I was in another room working on a report. Recognizing my father's bellowing voice from the cell block as he yelled at one of the cops, I felt a jolt of adrenaline and tears welling in my eyes. I got up and spoke with my supervisor, asking him if I could go home. He mercifully nodded his head and okayed my request. I changed into my civilian clothes and left the police station, crying all the way home.

It was one of the most humiliating experiences of my life. It turned out that my father was evaluated and sent home with new medication. It never really corrected his behavior, but it was effective in establishing future boundaries. He no longer fought with neighbors, and he never again needed police intervention to mitigate his behavior. I was grateful that the officer who served the warrant to my father was an older, experienced, and compassionate man, Dave Arsenault, who was understanding and willing to help in this seemingly impossible situation.

Having met many people who profess patriotism, I find it baffling how many of these flag wavers are so ignorant about the cost of war and military service. They neglect to acknowledge the invisible scars left on those who served, their families, and their descendants. The trauma experienced by service people in many instances is passed on from one generation to another.

I came to realize that these same dynamics of generational trauma were also present in my own community. I witnessed firsthand how families, mostly people of color, had been crippled by the long-term effects of poverty and substance abuse, two of the most insidious causes of crime in our community. And in the mid-1980s and early 1990s, the financial realities in Fitchburg made it impossible to impact change and make improvements on a systemic level.

Despite the flaws in our system, the field of policing experienced a renaissance of sorts upon the election of President Bill Clinton and his promise to put 100,000 new cops on the street as part of his policy to address growing crime in our country. Clinton's re-envisioning of public safety was the catalyst nationwide for sweeping changes to policing. On the plus side,

Clinton's policies put a new emphasis on community policing and preventative measures in law enforcement. It cannot be ignored, however, this was also responsible for the disproportionately high number of arrests and convictions for people of color.

    As fate would have it, I was promoted to the position of sergeant around this time. My first promotion was well received by my fellow officers who saw both my wealth of hands-on experience and the fact that I had paid my dues, serving nine years on the street. I was now in a position not only to lead but to participate in the most massive overhaul in policing since its modern foundation two hundred years ago. Federal funds began to flow into cities and towns to facilitate the implementation of community policing in all areas of our country. Fitchburg, however, continued to suffer from economic distress and crime, namely due to a lack of tax revenue. The one silver lining of this problem was that when it came time to seek financial assistance, the police department received a large grant from the Department of Justice under their new COPS (Office of Community Oriented Policing) office. In order for the city to receive this funding, the Fitchburg Police Department had to agree to send two supervisors to a conference sponsored by the federal government to learn about community policing. I was selected to attend along with another supervisor.

    The conference emphasized the true meaning of community policing. It highlighted a bottom-up approach to solving crime problems and empowering line officers to create powerful partnerships with the community they served in order to enlist their support. This training was in deep contrast to and in conflict with the heavily ingrained paramilitary approach of policing over the decades: that police alone were responsible for solving crime and for providing safety in our communities.

My colleague and I returned to the department reinvigorated and energized to help bring about change in our community. After learning about these new and exciting strategies for creating partnerships and developing relationships within the community, we were quickly deflated when the administration told us that there was no way they would implement this kind of policing. This was one of the first undeniable signs that my future at the Fitchburg Police Department was in doubt.

Once again, I channeled my passion for knowledge and innovation in law enforcement into my education. After receiving my bachelor's degree from the University of Massachusetts Lowell, I opted to continue my studies while the momentum was still behind me by applying for acceptance into their master's degree program.

Undeterred by the resistance to change in my own department, I funneled my energies into my academics. With the help of my mentor and department chairperson, Dr. Eve Buzawa, I was afforded an opportunity to take my criminal justice education and my interest in community policing to another level. In August of 1993, Dr. Buzawa invited me to attend Oxford University in England where I would take two graduate courses on the British Criminal Justice System. I only had to supplement my travel expenses. Even room and board at the college was included in the price. I was also able to bring my wife, Sue with me, and this allowed us to expand my studies into a European vacation.

I could not pass up such a great opportunity. The only issue I had to resolve was how I was going to take time off from work. Certain that I could not use vacation time, I decided to approach my department and ask if this could be considered as professional development. Our police chief at the time was a disciplinarian and was quite strict, but he was also a tremendous proponent of police training. The chief knew that I took my job in policing very seriously and always put forth good effort. I was hopeful that he might be willing to allow me this unique educational experience.

I wrote up the training request and submitted it to my chief in person. Much to my surprise and delight, the chief immediately gave me his authorization to go. A man of few words, he never articulated why he approved my request, but his actions were clear. He knew me to be a good, honest police officer, and I was being rewarded. This opportunity also brought a certain level of prestige to the department. This was the first time that a police officer from Fitchburg was gaining this type of international experience.

I found out a short while later that another officer had put in for an educational training request and was quickly denied. It was then that I learned a new meaning to the old saying in policing that, "It all depends on who you are." In this case, I was afforded an opportunity because I did the right thing. This time it meant that if you are really good at what you do then exceptions can be made. I was off to England.

Chapter 6

Oxford: What I Thought I Knew

Landing in London Heathrow Airport after an overnight transatlantic flight from Boston, I had mixed feelings of exhilaration, good fortune, and exhaustion. These feelings were combined with mental fogginess as I tried to figure out how to get the bus to Oxford. My wife, Sue, and I finally managed to buy two bus tickets after figuring out what the ticket seller was saying in his cockney London accent. We then waited for a couple of hours after dragging our luggage across the massive airport and finding the bus station.

It was summer and the weather was sunny and comfortable on that midmorning. A strange feeling of warmth mixed in with my jet lag. After climbing on board the bus, and lifting our large over-packed suitcases, we were finally seated. Fighting off the urge to sleep, the two-hour bus ride passed fairly quickly, stopping at two prior destinations before we ended up in downtown Oxford. The bus took us to High Street, the main thoroughfare of the city, right in front of

Queens College where I would be staying and attending my classes.

Barely able to move, Sue and I were kindly assisted by an English gentleman who took pity on us and helped us off the bus with our luggage. There we stood on this busy street looking up at the beautiful, ancient stone gates of the college, founded in 1341, and named for Queen Philippa, the wife of King Edward III. Attached to the ancient gates was a medieval stone guard house attended by the porters of the college, English gentlemen in black suits and ties. They moved and spoke with an attitude of superiority that conjured up scenes from old Hollywood movies of British royalty.

It was obvious that "we were not in Kansas anymore," so we decided to play along with the current scenario, and informed the porters of our arrival, and requested a room at the college. Moments later, Sue and I were escorted across the emerald grass of the historic quad to a spartan room in the two-story dormitory on this small campus. Sue and I looked at the two twin beds in our room and immediately pushed them together to make one bed. After quickly cleaning up, we both immediately fell unconscious on our bed, taking comfort in our venerable, but humble quarters for the next two weeks.

Rising the next morning, we made our way to the dining hall. Walking through the beautifully manicured main courtyard accented by stone architecture designed by Sir Christopher Wren left me with the feeling of being a misplaced interloper. I shortly learned that Oxford University was made up of 39 small colleges like this one, quite different from the mega universities associated with greatness in the United States.

The ambiance of these historic grounds made us feel like we were walking through an ancient museum, and I was overwhelmed by a feeling of privilege to have such a unique opportunity. When we entered the dining hall, we met some of the other twelve students who had arrived from the US to take part in this intensive program studying the British Criminal Justice System. It was reassuring to meet fellow students and we quickly became acquainted while eating our English breakfast beans and ham.

I was delighted to discover that our student delegation included another police officer from Medford, Massachusetts, Paul Mackowski, and his wife Mary. We immediately hit it off and we spent much of our downtime together as couples. The rest of the students were much younger, primarily graduate students, who were continuing their studies immediately after attaining their bachelor's degree.

While we were all conversing, I found out that students had been arriving at different times. Some had already been at the university for a couple of days. One young woman told us of her first harrowing night sleeping in the dorm. She was in her bed asleep when she was awakened by the rattling of the outside doorknob of her locked room. The disturbance continued for several minutes, and she managed to call the main desk to inform them of a possible intruder. She explained a short while later that she heard the heavy footsteps of what she believed to be a prompt response to her request. The rattling at her door had stopped.

She then went to her door and cracked it open, looking into the dimly lit hallway. She saw a young man in his early twenties, swaying on his knees, trying to place a key into a dorm door. He was clearly intoxicated and confused, and he had moved onto another room after finding out his key did not fit her door lock. She explained that she saw an indignant porter standing over him, exclaiming, "You bloody peasant bastard!" Turns out it was one of our American graduate students after a night out sampling the Oxford pubs. This was not exactly a stellar reflection on the quality of our group.

Despite the jet lag and lack of sleep, we immediately began our classes that morning. Sitting in an ancient classroom, I got my first taste of an Oxford education as the Don immediately started into a monotone lecture on the history of British law. "Don" was the title given to professors at Oxford who were senior faculty members of their departments. It was a word signifying respect for knowledge and accomplishment. I listened as carefully as my travel-wracked body and mind would allow.

The Don read from his notes at a fairly rapid speed. First, he informed us that we were in the country of the United Kingdom, which consisted of England, Scotland, Wales, and Northern Ireland. Then he began talking about English Common Law and I soon became lost. My mind was working overtime trying to process and absorb all of this new information and different terminologies delivered in a thick English accent. I raised my hand to ask a question, requesting further explanation of a term he used. It was then that he stared at me and announced there would be no questions during his presentation; that we could ask questions when he was finished. This was my first lesson in classroom etiquette in England, which was quite unlike my experience at American universities, where questions were always encouraged.

I was reminded that the presenter here was the expert and that it was our duty and responsibility as students to quietly absorb the information as a whole and then ask questions. It was different but, in a way, it made sense. Listen to the expert. My first lesson learned.

We soldiered on and met one of the other professors, a young affable Irish gentleman named Ian. Unlike the Don, Ian was more relatable and excited to interact with American students. Ian was a welcome relief from the stuffy, haughty lecture of a Don. A specialist in the evolution of probation and corrections in the United Kingdom, Ian was also a thorough researcher. While he employed a lecture style similar to a Don, Ian created a much more relaxed classroom environment, and proved to be more in tune with our group. I believe he even went out and hoisted a pint or two with some of the students.

Included in our educational program was a chance to see the British criminal justice system in action. Midweek, I was given the opportunity to do a ride-along with the Thames Valley Police, the regional arm of the UK national police force. I was assigned to a friendly and informative police officer who was about my age. We drove through mostly rural areas while discussing the differences between our systems of law enforcement.

I shared with him my frustration with investigating juvenile crimes, especially house breaks. I told him that after the first time I arrested a juvenile, he was taken to court and predictably given probation. In the proceeding weeks, the same juvenile would be charged again, and this time brought to court and given a suspended sentence. It was only after the third time that the subject was apprehended again that the court would move to assign the juvenile to some form of detention. The reality of the situation was that even though the suspect had been caught three times, that suspect probably had wreaked havoc by committing more than twenty other housebreaks for which they were not charged or held responsible.

    The British police officer lamented a similar situation he encountered regarding car thefts by youth. In the British system, the youth is summoned to the police station along with their parents and informed of the charge, then a discussion begins on some form of remediation. The parent conference became part of the written record if the matter needed to be brought to court in the future or if there was a subsequent offense. This intrigued me because the police action taken prior to court was part of the written record of the offender. It could be seen and evaluated by a judge even if the person was not previously formally charged. This process would not be legal back home. It would not be until 2022 while I was taking a course called Foundations of Restorative Practices online that I would meet a former officer of the Thames Valley Police who informed me that they were using restorative justice practices back in 1993 when I was in Oxford.

    In the United States, each offense needs to be dealt with only on the merits of the individual case and not on prior history or knowledge. Clearly, the British form of government and their constitution were quite different from ours. The system of justice in the United States was not perfect, and it was clear to me that we could learn quite a bit from other countries. The British system of law's use of parent conferencing for dealing with juvenile offenders would work much better for both the victims and the perpetrators and could alleviate a large volume of unnecessary cases taking up the court's time.

As we continued to drive, I asked the obvious question that any American police officer would ask: "How do you do your job without carrying a gun?" He nonchalantly answered that it was not in the tradition of British police, in the way that they worked and interacted with the public.

"What happens in the event of something violent?" I immediately asked.

He described British police protocol, that there were always two-person police vehicles on the road with firearms in the trunk that could be promptly engaged if a situation called for it.

Being a young police officer from America, I was uncomfortable with his answer. But after further thought and contemplation, it made sense. This was a different country, where firearms were not revered. The United States had been steeped in the tradition of firearms throughout its history, exemplified by slogans like "The gun that won the west," or "An armed society is a polite society." The topic the availability of firearms in society will always be a debatable and contentious issue in America.

But clearly, what is not debatable is the horrific amount of gun violence in America, astronomical murder rate, and the deplorable number of police officers killed in the line of duty by firearms in the United States as compared to the United Kingdom. As many as 50 police officers a year are killed by firearms in the United States while the number in the UK is in the low single digits. Also, police are averaging almost 1,000 fatal shootings a year in the U.S. compared to single digit numbers in the UK.

This conversation with my British colleague provoked deep reflection on my part. Despite the deep differences in laws and methodologies, the cold, stark contrast of the numbers listed by both countries cries out for explanation and rethinking of our violent culture in the United States, regardless of political point of view. The statistics mentioned above are just the tip of the iceberg of our gun problem in America.

I noticed another big cultural difference when lunch time rolled around. We drove to the local precinct house. Upon arrival, I noticed a much more informal and relaxed atmosphere than at the station back home. I was led through the lobby to an adjacent room. When I entered, my jaw dropped. Right there in front of me was a full-blown British pub actually inside the police station premises where drafts of ale were being poured.

Stunned, I looked at my UK colleague in disbelief. "Are you allowed to have a beer with your meal?"

"Yes, of course," he answered, in a nonchalant way. His response shocked me. Again, I was startled by the odd civility of the custom of having a beer with one's meal while on duty as a police officer. The contrast with my American experience was more than jarring. Alcohol has been so abused and misused in our American culture. Sadly, the last time I saw a beer for on duty police consumption was a Miller Light beer can rolling out from under my seat as I was applying the brakes in my police car.

My hands-on learning about the British Criminal Justice System would close out by a visit to the local court. The courts on a local or district level proved to be also quite different from those in the United States. I was taken into a very packed small courtroom where I could barely stand without feeling the crush of bystanders around me. I listened as the court barrister spoke loudly and authoritatively with his eyes scanning the room as he spoke. There was a haughtiness about him that turned me off, and when his eyes met mine, he stared hard at me, noting my displeasure in his demeanor. Not knowing much about the court system, I chalked this experience up to cultural differences between authoritative British formality, and the more humble and unassuming stature of a common Yank from the United States.

However, some of the traditions and methods of the British court system did fascinate and impress me. Unlike the Massachusetts court system where a judge can listen and decide a case if the offender does not choose a jury trial, the "judges" in these lower-level cases in the British system consist of a panel of three retirees or pensioners from the community. The legal proceeding of the court itself is run by a legal barrister who keeps order and notes points of law. I also learned that the "judges" were constantly rotated with new people from the community.

I came away impressed that the British system had such a direct connection to the lives of the local citizens. This was just another example to me that there are better systems in the world, and that the American system is not always the best. It also opened my mind to thinking about *what could be* rather than just accepting *what is.*

Our time in Oxford was coming to an end and my wife, Sue, arranged for me to have cake in a beautiful

English flower garden to celebrate my 40th birthday. We closed out our stay in England with a fabulous weekend in London, attending three theater performances and sightseeing in this storied European capital. We returned home not knowing what would happen next. It did not take long to find out as I encountered something unforeseen and career changing.

Chapter 7

Russia: Shock and Awe

The plane shook as we touched down on the runway at the Russian military base outside Petrozavodsk in May 1994. Our delegation of 26 American police officers landed in the northwest region known as Karelia.

The plane wheels screeched several times as we slowed to a roll and began taxiing. We could feel the jolt of an uneven, rutted runway as we came to a full stop after passing a couple of parked MIG fighters and several airplanes in various stages of dilapidation. The plane doors opened while we were still on the runway, piquing our curiosity.

Walking down the stairs out of the plane, I realized that there were no terminal or gates. Continuing down the stairs, I heard a loud diesel engine sound and looking to my right, I saw an ancient World War II-style green bus billowing large, thick clouds of black smoke from an overhead exhaust pipe. The body of the bus was dirty, with heavy rust and holes along both sides. My fellow travelers and I looked on in stunned silence at the crumbling scenes of a once powerful Cold War adversary. We were further puzzled when we were greeted by the police and custom officials who processed our passports at an old desk sitting outside near the runway.

The uniformed woman who processed us had a very formal, official demeanor despite the backdrop of the primitive surroundings in which she was working. This scene became a metaphor in my mind of what a sham the Soviet Union was, spouting their propaganda without the ability to actually enhance peoples' lives or living conditions. This airport was living proof.

There were many American service veterans in our group. Several of them served in Vietnam. The consensus among them later was the thought that this is what we were afraid of all those years.

The journey to understanding how these events had unfolded began after I returned from Oxford in the summer of 1993. Arriving home and back to work from Oxford on the following Monday morning seemed normal enough. I dropped off the souvenirs I had purchased in England to the chief and captain with heartfelt gratitude for the opportunity to travel, and I resumed my duties as street supervisor in the patrol division. It wasn't long before I received a phone call from my colleague, Paul, from the Medford Police Department who had studied with me at Oxford.

Paul explained that he was interested in another international trip, this time to Russia. The collapse of the Soviet Union and its effects were still largely being felt around the world. It was a time of new promise in Russia. After struggling for many years in a failed communist system, there was a feeling of new-found hope, a sense that anything was possible.

Paul was creative and entrepreneurial, and possessed a deep fascination with and a desire to visit Russia. He wanted to lead the first delegation of American police officers to this once forbidden and mysterious country that engaged the US in a Cold War dominated by threats of mutual nuclear destruction. He said that he had family roots in Eastern Europe, and now that the Soviet Union had broken up, he wanted to take American cops on an exchange visit.

Prior to joining the force in Medford, Paul had worked in a small police department in Vermont. He learned about a focused non-profit organization there that facilitated professional exchange groups between musicians and teachers with Russia. Paul was hoping to approach the group and gauge their interest in arranging for a group of police officers from the US to visit Russia.

My response to Paul at first was less than enthusiastic. He had mentioned it when we were in Oxford and I had dismissed it as impracticable and, at best, a fantasy. But Paul was not to be dissuaded. Not only was Paul still interested in doing the exchange program, but his enthusiasm had elevated to the point of becoming infectious, so I decided to support the idea.

Agreeing to approach our contacts in our respective regions of Massachusetts, he in the eastern part of the state, and me in the central region, we began recruiting interested participants. Paul connected with Project Harmony, the aforementioned non-profit that had been facilitating music and education exchange programs to Russia. They operated out of the tiny village of Waitsfield, Vermont and was founded by several insightful and creative local citizens.

Their purpose was to open channels of communication between people in both Russia and the United States. Project Harmony sought to find and nurture commonalities with opportunities to get to know each other and share their cultural experiences. The sponsored musicians and teachers from both countries were hosted by families, opening up new avenues of discussions at a time when the American and Russian governments were barely speaking to each other.

Paul reached out to Project Harmony and asked them if they would be willing to sponsor a police exchange. Project Harmony was very interested and agreed to sponsor Paul on an exploratory trip to Russia to propose his idea to the Russian police through Project Harmony's established government contacts. Paul traveled to Russia with one of his department colleagues and was able to work out the specifics to make this exchange program between the U.S. and Russian police a reality. The exchange program would be with a police department in Petrozavodsk, the capital city of the Karelia region.

Petrozavodsk was an industrial city of about 265,000 people located near beautiful Lake Onega. The word "Petrozavodsk" literally translates in English to "Peter's Factory," a reference to the city's history during the time of Peter the Great in the 1700s when it became a major foundry and manufacturer. Its geographical location on the border of Finland made for a very complicated history of war and occupation. Petrozavodsk, or Petroskoi as the Finnish call it, had once been part of Finland, but was finally ceded back to

Russia as a result of World War II. Interestingly, because of the fall of the Soviet Union, many Finnish people living in Karelia were now being offered full repatriation to Finland and were being financially supported by the Finnish government to do so.

  I also learned from Project Harmony that Karelia was situated at a great distance from centralized Moscow. This distance resulted in a more autonomous local government that was open to exchanging ideas with Americans. They were not as controlled by the adversarial politics that existed between our two countries. Being a long-time history and political junkie, the more I learned about this region, the more attractive this opportunity was becoming. I realized that our systems of policing would be very different, but the experiences of being a police officer and confronting human behavior was similar and created a natural bond that could build relationships based on shared experiences.

  Paul returned from his exploratory trip and informed me that the Russians had greeted him with open arms. They were very enthusiastic about the American police coming to Petrozavodsk. This news sold me on my participation in this exciting opportunity. It wasn't long before I mentioned the idea to a couple of fellow officers in my police department who immediately said they wanted to go and participate. Before I knew it, several officers in my region were contacting me to sign up. All the expenses associated with the trip were assumed by the officers themselves. The local press heard about the initiative and began contacting us for interviews. The reporter who interviewed us from the Sentinel and Enterprise, the local newspaper, signed up for the trip. Eventually,

Paul had raised the interest of a major national television network that decided to join us and document our trip for national viewership. It seemed the story itself had become much larger than the efforts we had put into it.

Paul managed to recruit police officers from New York City, Boston, and Denton, Texas. After recruiting a total of 28 participants, our next step was to meet the staff from Project Harmony. All the local participants who signed up for the exchange program were invited to attend a briefing and orientation put on by Project Harmony at the Medford Police Station. The purpose of the meeting was two-fold: first, to give us a cultural orientation of current life in Russia, and second, to identify and prepare a criminal justice presentation on American policing to share with our Russian counterparts. Project Harmony's hope was that this exchange program would bring about a new dialogue between police officers from two different worlds, resulting in the sharing of professional knowledge and experiences, as well as forging new conversations and friendships that would last a lifetime.

Project Harmony did fantastic work organizing the logistics of our trip, providing interlocutors and interpreters for our meetings and presentations. Their groundbreaking work was all based on high ideals of peace and understanding and the invaluable connections they had established over the years in Russia. Project Harmony's values and people were of the highest integrity and goodness. It was truly the most dynamic and altruistic organization I have ever worked with.

After completing the orientation and travel logistics, we were off to Russia in early May of 1994.

After we landed and our documents were processed, we were taken to a municipal building in Petrozavodsk where we were officially welcomed by the Russian police. We were brought into a large room and were officially and warmly greeted by our Russian hosts. A sense of wonder and the excitement of discovery was in the air as our Project Harmony staff translated for our delegation. All the Americans were standing on one side of the room and the Russian host families were on the other side. Our names were called off individually and we were introduced to our host families and taken to our host apartments where we would be staying for the next two weeks.

My experience involved living with a fellow Russian police officer who was a detective like me. He lived in a concrete Soviet built high-rise apartment building that had fallen into disrepair. These buildings had been hurriedly built during the housing crisis in the former Soviet Union over the last twenty years. The apartments were very small and the whole building had one central heating system for dozens of apartments. The evidence of decay, both social and economic, were evident in simple things, like lights burnt out in unclean hallways and lobbies.

My host, Alexander, or "Sasha," as he preferred to be called, informed me that things had gone downhill the last couple of years as the Soviet Union fell apart due to terrible economic conditions. Lines at food stores were common and everything was either rationed or in short supply. Yet here he was, welcoming me into his home and sharing what little he had. I was immediately humbled by his family's graciousness and kindness and would learn that sharing in this way negated any political difference and made us all human beings who cared about and loved our families.

During our orientation from Project Harmony before leaving the U.S., I had learned that oftentimes a member of your host family would have to sleep in the living room and give up their bed for you. I was conscious of the time and always retired early so that the teenage daughter in my apartment could get a good night's sleep before school in the morning.

People in this society were suffering due to shortages of simple products that were just not available. It was common to find toilet seats missing in public restrooms, as they were often stolen and brought home to use in an apartment. Also missing from most restrooms was toilet paper, and instead there would be a newspaper or a magazine that could be used to finish up after using the bathroom.

Alexander had a car. It was a small basic Lada that evolved from the Italian manufacturer, Fiat, but was manufactured in Russia without improvements from year to year. Alex was lucky to even have this vehicle, as there was a long waiting list to get one of these cars. The scarcity of cars and motor vehicle parts was evident when Alex would park outside his building. He would get out of the car and remove the windshield wipers as these were often stolen if they were carelessly left on the vehicle overnight.

A short time after we arrived home in the evening, dinner would be served. I remember the food being well cooked by his wife. I enjoyed the pleasant company of his teenage daughter who spoke enough basic English to enable us to have some limited conversations. In my chats with Alexander's family, I mentioned that I was Catholic, and I wanted to know if there were any services available to attend in the city. He did not directly answer my question but did mention to me that he and his family had all been baptized in the past. I found this intriguing as I learned through schooling and the media during the cold war era that religion of any kind was not allowed in the Soviet Union. Remembering my orientation suggestions, I announced that I would retire early because of my jet lag.

    The next morning started with a cup of coffee. It was not the Dunkin' Donuts variety but rather European or Turkish style coffee better known as espresso. I had never tasted this kind of coffee before, but needing my morning boost, I tried this short cup of concentrated, bitter coffee that was boiled in a metal cup over the stove. After sweetening the espresso with sugar, I almost liked it. We finished breakfast and began our first day of working together.

    Alex was a detective at the police department. He brought me to a large room where I would meet with my American colleagues. We spent the first part of the morning comparing notes as to our living circumstances and our observations of our host families. We then divided up and partnered with Russian police officers to learn about their work. During our first day, the American officers also delivered several presentations on police work in our country. My presentation was on the raging AIDS epidemic. My goal was to present the history of the disease, understanding how it was spread and how to protect oneself against being infected.

    Prior to going to Russia, I had submitted my presentation proposal and was told that no one would be interested in learning about AIDS as this problem didn't exist in Russia. I stood my ground and said that I wanted to go forward with the presentation. When I finally gave the presentation, it was of interest as it was information that the Russian police officers had never heard before. One of the officers did state that AIDS was not yet a problem, but I reminded him that with the end of the Cold War, many different people would be traveling to Russia which could subsequently result in the arrival of AIDS at their doorstep. This information seemed to be well received.

At the end of the day, Alex met me in the gathering room with the other American officers. He escorted me out to his car, and we drove for a short while before he turned down a street and came to a stop in front of a plain stone building. He motioned for me to get out of the car and to follow him. I walked with him to the front door and entered. Much to my astonishment, there was a Catholic mass in progress being delivered in Russian. I found my way to a seat and began to follow the liturgy. It was in a different language, but I knew the words and began to pray.

After a short while, Alex tapped me as I was bent over kneeling and nervously indicated to me that we had to leave. I sensed that this was not a good place for him to be seen, but I deeply respected him for taking the time to find this service for me. Although the Soviet Union was officially disbanded, there were still many strong elements of Soviet tradition and behaviors present. I thanked Alex and we left.

Most of the time spent in Russia consisted of our delegation giving presentations on American policing methodology and learning about Russian policing, both in practice and its history. The police here were called the militia or *militza* and are considered a branch of the military. After we did our presentations, we fielded questions and answers from our host officers.

The most common question was "What is your salary?" It wasn't long before we learned that police in Russia made one hundred dollars a month, and many had not been paid on a regular basis as there was not enough money being sent from the centralized government in Moscow. We were shocked to learn that even though the police had cars they usually did not take them to calls as gasoline was too expensive. Shockingly, officers would often take the trolley bus to get to their calls. We heard many of these stories and were astonished by the fact that these officers still showed up for work despite the lack of financial compensation. It was humbling for us to learn about their reality knowing how well we were compensated for our work at home.

During our stay, we were guests at many lavish banquets. These spreads had an array of offerings, some delicious foods and some not so familiar to our western palates. I was not a big fan of caviar, red or black, and it was always offered during our meals outside our home. Caviar is a delicacy in Russia and offering this luxury to our group was a way of honoring our presence. Again, this was so impressive for us as it was apparent that the average Russian could not afford it, nor did they eat like this very often.

One constant offering in both our outdoor gatherings and in our hosts' apartments was vodka. Toasts were a common occurrence at all meals and a nice tradition for people to speak from the heart. Many toasts extolled the joining of Americans and Russians together after years of tension, fear, and misunderstanding. It was a regular theme of glad tidings that prevailed throughout our visit and beyond.

On the free weekend during our stay, I spent time outdoors with Alex and his family. They had a dacha, or small country house, outside the city that was a much enjoyed and welcome retreat for them away from the crowded urban city. I will never forget fetching water from a well with a large wooden pole and bucket. My fellow officers and I visited several rural dachas. This was where Russians escaped the grittiness of city living to renew their spirits and reconnect with nature. It also provided sustenance for their daily living as most grew vegetable gardens that supplemented their family meals.

We met up with a few of the other officers in the American delegation and their host families and ate *shashleek*, a Russian style of barbeque, consisting mostly of pork. It was delicious. During this gathering, we learned that we would be served a special dish for us on this occasion. My host pointed to a large, metallic pot boiling over an open fire. I gazed into the pot and noticed a swirl of vegetables simmering in a broth along with large pieces of fish, including the heads. I learned that this soup was called *ohra*. A short time later, I was handed a large bowl of fish soup, fortunately without the fish head. I feigned appreciation for this wonderful meal and managed to scoop a spoonful of white fish that I put in my mouth. Biting down, I noticed a full side of fish bones on the meat and exclaimed, "The fish has bones in it!"

"Of course, fish has bones in it," my host casually responded.

We ended our weekend touring the beautiful island of Kiji located on Lake Onega where we visited a restored ancient wooden monastery.

Our last week consisted of doing more presentations and riding with the Russian police. After one of our presentations, I was speaking with an older Russian police officer who reminded me that during the Vietnam war, Russians sometimes piloted North Vietnamese fighter jets and dueled with American pilots. On a later trip to Russia, one Russian police officer hugged one of the Vietnam vets in our group and apologized for any harm that his country had done to the United States. Several of our American participants related similar stories from their Russian counterparts.

This trip was a professional experience of a lifetime, but the real measurable goodness of this adventure was the relief felt by all participants that we are all human, that we all had similar human cares and concerns, and that we were all glad to put the past behind us. We finished up our trip with a sumptuous banquet at a local restaurant near the lake. The dinner went late into the evening. I remember leaving the restaurant around midnight with the sun glaring brightly.

We soon returned home to the United States and learned that our new Russian colleagues would be coming as a group to the United States in the fall. We would host them, as they had done for us, staying with our families. We would arrange a program for their officers as well as a cultural experience that included visiting Washington, DC.

Because the Russian police officers were severely handicapped by lack of funds, our police group did a fundraiser, a casino night, run by our police association in Fitchburg to help defray the costs. The Russian police delegation of about 25 arrived in October of 1994 and along with hosting them in our families, we put together a program on American policing that included ride-alongs with American police officers on actual calls, a visit to our police academy, participation in firearms training, and a visit to the nation's capital, and the first ever visit of a Russian police delegation to the FBI Academy. We attended a presentation at the academy and were greeted by the FBI Director, Louis Freeh, who did a nice photo shoot with the delegation.

After the photo opportunity, our group was surprised by a representative of the U.S. State Department who expressed a great interest in our program. Project Harmony would have further talks with the International Narcotics and Law Enforcement (INL), the branch of the State Department which eventually ended up funding four more police exchange programs in the next four years for officers from Oryol and Volgograd, Russia as well as Odessa and Lviv, Ukraine. The police exchanges followed the same format with American police paying their own way and Former Soviet Union police officers' expenses paid for by the US State Department.

There were many remarkable moments during these four years, but nothing left a greater impression on me more than our time spent in Volgograd, the modern-day name of the city of Stalingrad. Stalingrad had been very likely the most pivotal battle of the Second World War.

We had arrived there with a contingent of 25 American law enforcement professionals in this city located on the Volga River. Like the rest of Russia, it was in a tumultuous transition from a former Soviet state to experimenting with western capitalism. At this time, I was the head of the police delegation and rather than being hosted by a Russian police officer, my wife and I were given our own apartment. It also included a 24-hour guard outside of our apartment consisting of two police officers with machine guns.

The next day we were taken to the downtown area of the city for a tour. We encountered a group of about two to three hundred people marching with the flag of the Soviet Union headed for a rally to celebrate May Day, the greatest holiday of the Soviet era. Despite all the economic difficulties and realities, there were still some people who pined for the old days of communism.

In contrast to that scene, we were later hosted at a local restaurant for lunch. Much to our surprise, our hosts had taken us to a strip club. I think in some weird way they were demonstrating to us some of their new freedoms. Later in the day, we were shown an area in Stalingrad where the Germans finally surrendered. This took place in a Russian Department store where the German Field Marshall Paulus emerged and gave up. We were also taken to a small section of the city that was left bombed out and devastated as a memorial to the people who suffered and gave their lives defending their country. The remains of a tank factory were part of that area. Tanks were built during the fighting, and they would literally drive out of the factory and onto the battlefield of the city.

A later tour of the local museum was led by an older woman who had lived through the siege of Stalingrad. I was stunned as she showed us a photo of Russian citizens who were hanged in the city by the Germans. She explained that she had known these victims personally. Later, we visited an area of the city called *Mamaeth Gorgon*, a large hill that saw the final battle and defeat of the German army in Stalingrad.

Today there is an enormous statue of Mother Russia with her hand stretched out, leading the charge with a large sword in the other hand. The size of the statue dwarfs the Statue of Liberty. I was told that a small Russian car could drive a circle in the palm of its outstretched hand.

Seeing all this drama and history conveyed a feeling to me of the suffering that Russia had gone through during this war of annihilation, and I understood why Russians were so paranoid about ever having their country invaded again. These police exchange programs were fascinating for sharing professional experiences but it was learning about the depth of suffering and resilience of other people that made the deepest impression on me.

Project Harmony formalized our program with the name Law Enforcement Exchange Program or LEEP, and I was given the title of assistant director. I continued to lead American police delegations to Ukraine and Russia over the next four years while continuing my duties as a law enforcement officer. These exchange experiences provided a tremendous amount of exposure to me as a leader of our delegations and emphasized the continuous importance of a grassroots program like this. The stories, experiences, and people I met through the years on these programs could fill another book.

CHAPTER 8

Gardner Police: Careful What You Ask For

Being a co-founder and leader of the police exchanges to the former Soviet Union was not only fascinating, gratifying, and unique, it also had the unintended effect of instilling new leadership skills in me. Partnering and organizing with Project Harmony necessitated the ability to recruit American police officers to participate and convince them to pay for their own way. In return, they had to host their Russian counterparts when they came to the U.S. I was representing American policing to the Russian government, and in essence, representing the United States.

During the first two years that these trips occurred, there was a tremendous amount of press coverage in both countries. As mentioned earlier, the first trip culminated with a major US television news agency covering our first visit to Russia and reporting it out on a popular national news show. While we were there, we experienced similar national coverage by the

Russian press. The officers and organizers participated in regular media interviews, answering a myriad of questions, and offering explanations about our police exchanges.

These public interviews required I articulate the importance of Project Harmony's exchange programs. In one interview, I was asked how our work was affecting relationships between our countries. I responded by saying that peace begins with one person at a time. It was soon evident to all involved that our methods were effective, and that Project Harmony was an organization that could be trusted.

The early to mid-90s was a unique time in relations between Russia and the United States. The Berlin Wall had come down and both sides had entered a period of good feelings. Citizens were more open to understanding and learning about each other's cultures. Living with host families was a hallmark of this program, creating a unique bond between the exchanges. Participants not only shared professional experiences but were able to see first-hand how their host family lived. This truly underscored for all participants that, despite political differences, we have so much in common and we all want the best for our families and countries.

Project Harmony's exchange programs began to draw the interest of the U.S. State Department. They showed great interest in our program and eventually funded the exchange program to bring Russian and Ukrainian police officers to the U.S. to continue our programs. During this time, I was invited to visit the State Department several times with Project Harmony to provide updates and inform them about our program's successes and challenges.

All of these experiences outlined required leadership skills. Whether it was organizing trips, reporting to the U.S. State Department, or giving interviews to the media, I was being called upon as a representative and leader of this program. I found myself growing in confidence with all these new experiences and felt very comfortable in these roles. The opportunity to travel and work internationally provided me with a new lens through which to see both policing and myself.

It gave me pause as I reflected on my role in the Fitchburg Police Department. I had worked there for fifteen years and had risen to the rank of detective sergeant. Leadership in a civil service organization was not easy to define, as promotions are done through a state testing process that involves studying prescribed books and dedicating a large amount of time studying for the promotional exam. A combination of discipline and rote memorization skills go into being successful in this process.

I took the sergeant's test twice before I passed the third time. The first time I took it, I did not study at all and just wanted to see what it was like. I had worked just over two years on the job and felt woefully unprepared to take a key leadership position when I had so much to learn. The second time I took it, I did not put in the time necessary to study, and again, I did not pass. The third time, I put in a strong effort and scored a 96 and topped the test among all Fitchburg officers who took the exam. While I did put in the extra studying effort required to score high on the exam, I also had nine years on the job at that point, and I felt accomplished in my role as a police officer.

Although I could have put in minimal effort in doing my job to prevent and solve crimes and got by in the civil service system, I held myself to a higher standard and put in the extra time when necessary to accomplish my tasks. I came to realize that this was a form of intrinsic leadership that was actually more important than passing a test. This kind of leadership acknowledgement came from your peers who watched you work diligently over the years and knew the time and character that you showed when performing your duties. This resulted in a form of unspoken respect.

One evening in early summer after our second exchange visit to Odessa, Ukraine, I was riding back from Boston with some fellow Fitchburg police officers and their wives after attending a wedding in Chinatown. I casually mentioned that there was an opening for police chief in the small neighboring city of Gardner and that I was thinking about submitting an application for the job. Upon arriving home that evening, my wife Sue asked me why I would say that I was applying for this job in a tone that implied that I could never get the job.

I continued to mull over the idea of applying for that chief's job and at the last minute, I decided to apply. My daughter Jessica, a good student and writer, helped me to pull together a resume. I was able to hand deliver my application materials to the mayor's office two hours before the deadline to submit. A few days later, I heard from Gardner and was invited to interview for the position.

I showed up at the interview feeling that I had nothing to lose and that I would give it my best shot. This interview also gave me the opportunity to expand on many of the ideas I had learned about community policing that were impossible to implement in my present department. The panel was led by the mayor's assistant, Jim Kreidler, and a local judge, Tom Carroll, who I knew from appearing before him in court many times as a police officer.

The interview took place in front of a committee of eight people in the council chambers at Gardner City Hall. I fielded a series of questions, all of which I felt comfortable answering, particularly those about community policing. I was able to exploit my knowledge on the subject because of my excellent education at the University of Massachusetts at Lowell and Oxford University. I answered all questions put to me with confidence.

I was surprised by the last comment from Judge Carroll, who asked while looking at my resume, "What is this Queens College, Oxford University?"

I explained that it was a part of my master's degree program and explained that it had really open my eyes to how things could be done differently in policing. He nodded at me with a look on his face of inquisitiveness and approval. I was confident that I had responded well, and when I stood up to leave, I thanked the committee for their time and for "allowing me to stretch myself professionally."

I left the meeting and drove home to Fitchburg. I was home for no more than a few minutes when the phone rang. and I answered it. It was Jim Kreidler.

He said, "They want you. We're offering you the job."

Shocked isn't a strong enough word for the way I felt upon hearing this. My immediate thought was that I hadn't expected a phone call, never mind offering me the job. I was in sheer disbelief.

The first thing that came out of my mouth probably sounded a bit defensive as I responded with, "I need to think about it."

"We need to know now," Kreidler responded firmly.

I asked for 24 hours to consider the offer and to think it over, and he finally consented. Before he hung up, he had one final question for me.

"My only reservation about you was that comment you made at the end of the interview about stretching yourself. What did you mean by that?"

I quickly gathered my thoughts and told him that I was sincerely honored by the opportunity even to interview for the job.

"Okay," he said, and our conversation ended.

The first person I called when I got off the phone was my brother, Michael. Michael was a successful president of a local credit union to whom I always looked up. He was seven years older than I, and he was someone I could reach out to for trusted fatherly advice. His wife, Mariam, answered the phone and she handed it to Mike.

I told Mike what had transpired.

"Really!" Mike said, in a tone of strong approval.

I will always remember his response. I told him I was nervous about accepting the position as I had no police administrative experience and that it would actually be a slight cut in pay because I could not work overtime anymore.

"Don't worry about the money," Michael advised. "This job is going to open a lot of doors for you. I would take it if I were you. There is nothing like sitting in the chair and making the decisions."

I took that to mean that, based on my interview, the committee had great confidence in my abilities, and that it was time to grow and respond to this new challenge. It felt almost as if this leadership position had found me. I thanked Mike and hung up.

A little later, my wife arrived home and I informed her of the news. She was as shocked as I was, and she asked me what I was going to do. I told her that I was going to accept the offer. I called Kreidler back a short time later and accepted the job. He told me that the next step would be to meet with him and the mayor as soon as possible.

Having made my decision to accept the chief's position, the next order of business was to inform my employer, Chief Ed Gallant, that I was going to be leaving. I went to his office and asked his administrative assistant if he was available to speak with me. Her office was connected to his, and she called him. Chief Gallant responded right away and said, "Send him in."

He was seated behind his neat executive desk wearing a crisp white uniform shirt.

"What's up?" he asked, looking up at me.

I then came right out with it and told him that I had just taken the position of chief of police in Gardner and that I was giving my notice. He immediately took off his glasses and backed up in his chair with a stunned look on his face at this totally unexpected and surprising news.

His first reaction to me was not congratulations, but a warning, "Don't do it."

He had been chief for many years now in Fitchburg and knew the human costs on himself and family. I knew that Chief Gallant's words of caution translated into, "You will have troubles. You will not be liked by peers. And once you take this step forward, there's no going back."

I told him that I understood his reservations because I had them, too. I mentioned how I thought this opportunity would open other doors for me down the road and he replied, "It certainly will do that."

I explained to him that I did not feel that I could continue to grow by staying in Fitchburg. I told him I was just a Sergeant and there were no opportunities for promotion on the horizon.

He shook his head and said, "No, Eddy, you are very valuable to this department just the way you are."

Chief Gallant was not a man of many words. In admitting to me that I was valuable, he was speaking volumes. It dawned on me that while I had been a Sergeant in the police department for over six years, I had handled every situation that had confronted me, from riots, to murders, to natural and industrial disasters.

Without saying the exact words, Chief was telling me that he was confident that I was capable of handling any challenge or crisis put in front of me. He did not say those words to me, but I finally knew that was what he meant. When he realized that there was no changing my mind, Chief Gallant later sat me down and gave me his advice on being a police chief. I vividly remember his first piece of advice. He strongly urged that I establish a well-funded training account to educate and professionalize my department. The chief explained that it was only through education and training that a professional police department could be established. He had seen first-hand how training had made such a change in Fitchburg. I knew from personal experience that Chief Gallant valued professional development opportunities for his officers as he was the person that had granted my leave so that I could attend Oxford, that brief period of time that had completely altered the trajectory of my professional life.

I thanked the chief for his advice and told him how grateful I felt to have worked with him. When later the local newspaper asked him about my having accepted the Chief's position in Gardner, Chief Gallant commented, "Ed Cronin has integrity and a sense of caring about him." It was a compliment that I would always cherish.

A day later, I met with Jim Kreidler at City Hall in Gardner. He prepared me for my interview with the mayor. Jim explained that the mayor was a blue-collar guy and that he would be very straightforward. After our brief conversation, I went to the mayor's office. I approached his desk as he stood, and I reached out and shook his hand, introducing myself. The mayor quickly noted that I was the recommended pick from the search committee, and he congratulated me on taking the job. He mentioned that he had received some positive feedback from my references.

"We called Judge Gelinas. He's a very serious and respected man and he gave you a good recommendation."

I could see by the look on his face that he had enormous respect for the judge and that the judge's recommendation meant a lot to him.

With introductions behind us, both the mayor and Mr. Kreidler went into a detailed history of the Gardner Police. They explained that the department had been very troubled several years earlier, to the point that a commissioner had been brought in from the outside to run the department. The chief's position had been relegated to a powerless figurehead.

In time, a top-down study and assessment was performed on the Gardner Police Department. The author of the report was Robert Sheehan, a Dean of the Criminal Justice Program at Northeastern University at that time. The report documented a history of outrageous behavior by some officers of the police department as well as intrusive local politics. Sheehan's report ended with a list of recommendations to improve the department. As a result, the police chief was given a buyout package and he had retired.

The chief of police position in Gardner had been taken out of the civil service system, one that appointed chiefs based on a narrow, department-only exam for the position. This process subsequently opened the position up to anyone who qualified to apply. Hiring was done on a merit basis, with a committee selecting a qualified candidate after an interview and thorough background check. I would be coming in as the second chief selected by this merit-based process.

The preceding chief had done an outstanding job across the board. He had been successful in removing malignant officers. He also brought new training and programming to professionalize the police department which included creating a strategic response team (PRT), trained to do high risk arrests and entries into buildings. The PRT was probably not really a necessary asset for the police, but it had created the effect of raising morale and pride within the department. The chief had also started to implement community policing before he left to take a position in Texas. I heard many positive stories about him, and he was worshiped by the officers at the time he left. This left very big shoes for me to fill. I subsequently learned that I had been selected for chief because I had articulated a strong understanding of community policing and, because of my professional communication on that topic, I was thought to be the right person to continue to develop this type of programming.

It all seemed to make sense. I was told that I would be confronting an immediate problem. The deputy chief, who had applied for the job, was not selected. She had previously sued the department over her appointment as a civil service deputy chief and won. It became clear that relations between her and the administration were not exactly great.

After learning this information, I was told I would be hired at will without a contract. I would get a three-year appointment by the City Council after my name was submitted by the mayor. The union contract and civil service protection that I had enjoyed as a police officer in Fitchburg no longer existed for me. Rather than a union to fall back on, I had only myself and my job performance to keep my position intact. It was risky to say the least, but I was ready to try something new and I knew that there would be no turning back.

My first order of business was to meet with the deputy chief. I felt that having a successful relationship with her was essential to moving the police department forward. I met with Sandra at a coffee shop a day later. I introduced myself to her and she was polite, respectful, and reserved. Knowing that she had applied for the position, I was sure that she felt disappointed that she did not get the job. I told her that I needed her help to be successful as chief and she said she would do her best.

I eventually learned that Sandra was one of the first full time female police officers in the county, appointed back in the late 1970s. She had endured many discriminatory practices during the course of her career at a time when women were just entering the police field. It is not my place to list the incidents she was victimized by, but I don't think I could have been able to work through it the way that she had. One thing that was evident to me was that I would invest my time and effort to further develop her executive skills that, in turn, would benefit the police department.

As a new chief of police with no administrative experience, my great friend Chief Robert Cudak of the of the Westminster Police Department, reached out and offered to show me the ropes. I had met Bob two years prior when he joined me and other police officers on the first two police exchanges. During that time, he demonstrated a warm, generous heart to all. He was now coming forward to treat me as a peer and to help me in any way he could.

He took me to area chief meetings and introduced me to many people in a similar position. He was always available with advice when I encountered administrative and personnel issues with which I needed help in deciding. He was a man of great integrity, one of the most faithful friends I have ever had and one of the most successful police chiefs ever in the North County.

My first six months at the Gardner Police Department was the honeymoon phase. I was on a steep learning curve as I grew to understand how my new police department functioned and was getting to know my personnel. I was quite pleased with the depth of excellent supervisors that worked for me and quickly became comfortable with their decision-making process.

One unforeseen aspect of the job was getting used to the politics of my new position. I quickly learned that being an at-will employee with no union to fall back on required very thoughtful decision making. It was my job to keep constituents like the mayor, City Council, local citizens, and the police union at peace while keeping their trust intact. It was challenging at times, but I used integrity in my decision making even if it put me in difficult positions from time to time. I always felt that my integrity was not negotiable and if I lost my position because I would not compromise it, then so be it. As my father had taught me growing up, "You have to be able to look at yourself in the mirror after you make a decision."

My real purpose for becoming chief in Gardner would not emerge until the beginning of January 1996. I received a call at about seven in the morning at my house in Fitchburg from a police dispatcher. There had been a fire at a local housing complex and a woman had died. I told the dispatcher to notify the mayor immediately and I then got in my car and drove to work right away.

Upon arriving at the department, I learned that there was far more to the story than I had initially thought and been told. I found out that my officers had been called to the scene of the fire the night before. A couple had been involved in a domestic argument and yet both parties said there had been no assault. The woman involved had simply wanted her boyfriend to leave. They had both been drinking. The responding officers had told the boyfriend that he had to leave, which he agreed to do. He was warned by the officers that if he returned to the apartment, he would be arrested. My officers let the woman know that she could seek a restraining order in the morning at the court.

The boyfriend subsequently reported that he had gone to a neighbor's place and after returning to the apartment, discovered that there was a fire. He said that his girlfriend was in there and was unresponsive.

The police and fire department were called and responded. Forced to crawl beneath the suffocating smoke, the responding officer reached for the woman, still lying prone in her bed, and dragged her lifeless body out of the apartment. The fire department had arrived on the scene and helped the Gardner police officer administer CPR, but it was too late. The woman had died.

Upon getting the information, I decided to go to the scene of the fire. When I arrived at the apartment, the front door was open, and a police officer was posted at the door, as I learned that the apartment was now considered a crime scene. A subsequent homicide investigation was underway. Walking into the apartment, I was immediately struck by the sight of the soot covered walls. Knowing that the woman was found in the bedroom, I made my way through the blackened landscape.

In the bedroom, I was aghast to see a blackened room and bed with the stark white imprint of a body on a white sheet. This site identified the exact spot and posture the woman was in when she died. Further investigation by the state police and our department determined that the fire was purposely set by the boyfriend, and he was arrested later in the day for murder.

Upon returning to the police station, I spoke with the detective lieutenant who updated me on the case. He said that the arrested suspect denied that he had killed the woman, but the evidence was overwhelming. As we were talking, the arrested boyfriend was removed from a room and brought into the main area where we were working. I will never forget the smirk on his face and his pathetic laugh as he walked by us. He thought his arrest and interrogation was a big joke.

This tragic incident would serve to inform me of my mandate for the rest of my tenure as chief of police. Gardner was a small city of about 20,000 people with hardly any minority groups at the time. My first priority would be to implement community policing programs that would serve the needs of the citizens and build trust with our department.

While reaching out across the city, I was invited to be part of a community health task force and I began attending their meetings. There was a broad representation that included medical personnel as well as municipal employees from the school, fire, and police departments. During these meetings, I learned about a new report that had just come out called "The Gardner Health Study." It was a project based out of the local hospital that collected data on health issues within the city and the surrounding areas. To my surprise, domestic violence assaults against women were the number one health issue presented at the emergency room at the local hospital.

By getting out in the community and working with other partners in the city, I had discovered what a terrible and insidious problem domestic violence had become in our community. Had I not employed community policing strategies as a means of engaging the partners in the community, our police department would never have discovered the extent of this problem. I had a newfound sense of clarity about where I should be applying our resources. Coincidentally, the department and city had received a solicitation for a grant from the Department of Justice's COPS (Community Oriented Policing Services) office. The grant was called "Community Policing to Combat Domestic Violence."

I received a call from our grant writer from the Office of Community Development, Shaun Suhoski, to see if I was interested in applying for this and I immediately said yes. Shaun wrote a brilliant application for this highly competitive grant and soon the Gardner Police Department was the recipient of $90,000 from the Department of Justice. This was a considerable amount of money at that time, especially for such a small city. The basis for the grant was the compelling data collected from the recent Gardner Health Study. The funds received from the grant award were immediately utilized to continue our community collaborative approach to address domestic violence.

Heeding the advice of my former chief, money was allocated for professional development and education as we conducted domestic violence prevention that cross-trained emergency room nurses and police officers. The goal was to build strong relationships and communication in order to better serve victims of domestic violence. Police officers and ER nurses are well acquainted with each other and are constantly brought together around criminal cases that end up in the emergency room. Both share common experiences with the same kind of human behavior and always support and back each other up in times of need.

    Funding from the grant was partially used for domestic violence victims to receive follow-up visits after incidents had taken place to ensure their safety, and to provide further assistance if necessary. The grant funding also enabled us to hire a victim's advocate to work at the police station to provide immediate assistance, resources, and options to victims, while relieving officers of this duty. There was even enough money to establish a teen domestic violence prevention curriculum for the local high school.

    This program proved quite successful in enhancing services for victims and, more importantly, it underscored the gravity of the problem in the region. While I did not know it at the time, our response to the issue of domestic violence also served a preventative function, as well. Police traditionally served the role of responding to domestic violence incidents: they could make an arrest and get immediate help for the victim. But it is only with long-term prevention efforts that communities can see an actual change in behavior, and create a healthier, more productive population. Police are called upon to have a leadership role in this area.

    Working to establish a meaningful and lasting domestic violence prevention program was something that I was very proud to leave as my legacy when my time in Gardner came to an end. I was duly satisfied by the positive working relationship I had established with Deputy Chief Sandra Dines. It was obvious to me that Sandra had been through many struggles being a woman on the job and had fallen victim to the politics of the region. Considering that I had been selected for the chief's position over Sandra could have spelled disaster for our relationship, but it was quite the opposite.

While serving as chief, I exposed Sandra to as much executive training as possible, including inviting her to attend the International Association of Chiefs of Police (IACP) Conference in Orlando, Florida. I was grateful to the mayor for allowing me to bring her to the conference, as a city our size did not usually send two candidates. Sandra responded strongly to these varied opportunities and went from being isolated and ignored within the department to being my strong right arm, leading the way on many tasks and initiatives.

When I gave my notice to leave Gardner in 1998, the mayor was considering appointing Sandra to the chief's position. But it so happened that the neighboring city of Athol had already hired her as their new police chief. I was so proud of her and the way she had overcome her past obstacles and had developed into an excellent police executive. It was just at this time that a new opportunity to grow was presented to me by Project Harmony, the organization that I had worked with to facilitate police exchanges over the last four years.

The International Narcotics and Law Enforcement (INL) of the U.S. State Department was soliciting Project Harmony for a proposal to bring a domestic violence program to countries of the former Soviet Union. My good friend and co-director of the law enforcement exchange program, Charlie Hosford, asked for my input on this proposal. Thus, the "Domestic Violence Community Partnership Program" to the former Soviet Union was born.

The proposal was eventually accepted and funded by the State Department. I was subsequently offered the position as director of this program and humbly accepted this new challenge. As my brother Michael had said, the job in Gardner would open many doors for me, and I was about to discover doors that would bring my skills to other parts of the world.

My Photographic Journey

My friend and mentor Captain Joseph Carbone of the Fitchburg Police Department

My wife Susan and I with Dr. Ian O'Donnell in the quad at Queens College at Oxford University

Future Chief Ernie Martineau, Todd Deacon, Tom Daoust and Tim O'Brien from the Fitchburg Police joining me on police exchange program to Odessa, Ukraine in 2005

My Domestic Violence Team training with me in Vogograd, Russia in front of Mamayev Kurgan. (Formerly Stalingrad)

Chief Ed Cronin receiving 2011 International Chiefs of Police Award for Individual Achievement in the Field of Civil Rights

Sayra Pinto, my dear friend and leader of the Latino Coalition

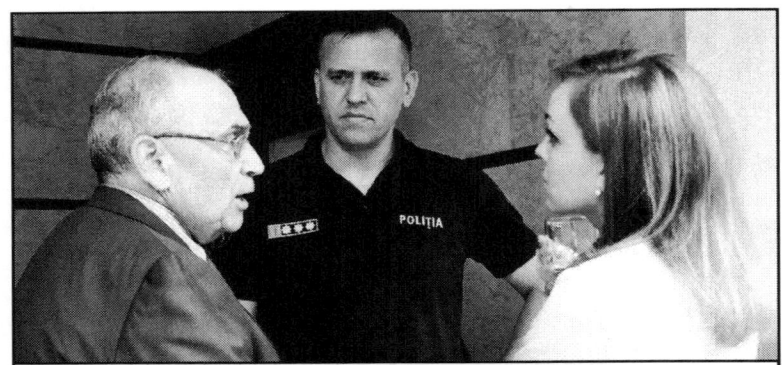

Chief Alexandru Pinzari with Myself and Valda Troian of the Border Police

IACP conference in San Diego, California with Chief Pinzari, Vladimir Kazacov, Vlada Troian, and Alex Molcean

Bike Patrol in Moldova

Dr. Carol Sharicz and I training on systems thinking at the Moldova Police Inspectorate in Chisinau

In front of the Great Pyramid in Giza, Egypt

My invaluable Sr. INL police advisor Alex Molcean whose work was indispensable to our success in working with police in Moldova

At Press conference with EU representative on police reform, Steven Daniëls and future Moldovan Minister of Internal Affairs, Ana Revenco

With Ulrica Granberg, Superintendent of the Swedish Police

Investigator Cristina Schimbov of General Police Inspectorate. First women police officer from Moldova to graduate from FBI National Academy

Women in Policing Conference in Tbilisi, Georgia

Adrian Ford; Director of Three Pyramids

IACP conference in Orlando, Florida with Khatia Dekanoidze

CHAPTER 9

Project Harmony: Taking It to the International Community

Standing in my living room, I surveyed the group of women in front of me and decided it was time to take a break. The small audience, while attentive and taking furious notes, had begun to shift in their seats. They seemed to breathe a collective sigh of relief when I said, "Let's take a ten-minute break. Grab a drink, use the bathroom. Whatever you need. Make yourselves at home."

The material we were covering for the Domestic Violence Community Partnership Program (DVCPP) was intense and likely burdensome to this crowd, many of whom had survived their own domestic violence situations. Moving through the room, I caught the eye of a woman who was seemingly staring at me. I gave her a friendly nod of acknowledgement, offered her a smile, and said, "I hope you're finding this information useful."

She gave me a once-over, looking me up and down, and coldly intoned, "Why the fuck are you in charge of this program?"

While I can't remember exactly how I responded to this trainer, a domestic violence expert, and a survivor herself, I can remember how I felt. I knew that as a man working in the field of domestic violence prevention, I had an uphill battle in front of me. I had to prove myself worthy of these women's trust. I had to show that I was not just another talking head, pretending to understand what these women had to endure. I had to earn their respect and their loyalty, and I knew this was a job worth committing myself to. And so began another bumpy journey towards growth and learning.

My time in Gardner had come to a close and I had just started in my new role as Director of the DVCPP. The first order of business was to recruit and develop my first group of trainers. This opportunity attracted many applicants from different fields of expertise, each of whom brought their own life experiences and personalities to this shared effort.

The trainer who questioned my leadership was a bright, educated woman who was highly skilled in delivering information on domestic violence. Many of the trainers seated in my living room for orientation that night were like her; exceptionally talented professionals who were on their own journey of healing. And this work in domestic violence prevention was a key component of their own empowerment, as they worked to reclaim what they had lost at the hands of their abusers.

I thought I understood domestic violence when I was studying with Dr. Eve Buzawa at UMass Lowell and when I was working at Project Harmony. But my experiences with domestic violence was at a scientific, non-empirical distance. In becoming the leader of the DVCPP, I was surrounded by survivors, both clients and employees, and my ultimate goal in this position was to gain their trust. It wasn't just data and statistics anymore; it was personal.

In early 1998, several months before leaving Gardner, I learned about this federal grant opportunity by Project Harmony. The First Lady, Hillary Clinton, made promoting women's programs around the world a key aspect of her political platform. After discussions with women in the former Soviet Union, she made a request to our government to fund programming to bring information and training on domestic violence to these countries. The INL was responsible for funding international police assistance programs and they began soliciting proposals from American non-governmental organizations (NGOs) that had experience in policing and work experience in these countries. Project Harmony was selected based on their years of police exchanges between Eastern Europe and the United States and because of their groundbreaking community approach to addressing domestic violence.

One of the directors of Project Harmony, Charlie Hosford, who had become my close friend and mentor, had asked whether I had any ideas that could be put into a grant application. I told him that the Gardner Police grant we received would be a perfect model for Project Harmony to follow. My first recommendation was to make it a community wide approach that included the police of the participating countries. Thanks to the goodwill established and the success of the law enforcement exchange programs, Project

Harmony had great connections to the police in participating countries and enjoyed their trust and dependability.

Having the police on board was a critical first step, as many of the former Soviet bloc countries still had the remnants of hierarchical governments that relied on top-down approval for new programming and initiatives into their countries. My experience in the U.S. and the west taught me that implementing a strong training program was imperative. Project Harmony would need to bring in domestic violence experts to address specific professional groups. For example, we would need to bring medical specialists on domestic violence to hospital personnel, EMTs, nurses, medical students, and others holding similar roles on our training trips. We also proposed to bring specialized trainers representing nonprofits, women advocacy groups, police, lawyers and legal professionals, psychologists and the education field.

There would be two rounds of training in each city selected to participate and at the end of the training cycles, the community groups and governmental organizations would be asked to form a coalition to prevent and support victims of domestic violence. In most communities, a resource center was established for victims of domestic violence to reach out for information and assistance after the program had ended. The grant was for a three-year period and involved conducting training and information programs to several cities in Russia, Ukraine and Georgia. Most of the cities selected were chosen because Project Harmony had done previous police exchange programs and had developed trust at these locations.

This trust was essential to being able to bring a program like domestic violence prevention and response to countries that had long operated under customs and traditions that had held women in subservient roles. From what I could tell, these cultures were also heavily influenced by Orthodox religion that prioritizes keeping families together despite incidences of abuse and suffering of women and children.

My own personal experience working with police of the former Soviet Union was that women had roles similar to U.S. policing back in the 1940s and 50s. They primarily dealt with children and females and were excluded from the traditional male roles of police response and investigative work. It was also obvious that many of the women in policing and in employment in society at large dressed in short skirts, high heels and heavy makeup and used their feminine image and attractiveness at work deliberately. On the other hand, it has been pointed out to me that women in these countries dressed this way to feel empowered because at least that was something they could feel good about and have control over.

These were obvious signs of differences that put women in these countries in a much different culture from women in western countries. They had not experienced a strong advocacy and successful movement of women's rights. On the other hand, culture in the former Soviet Union encouraged women to look beautiful at work; however, even if women dressed in a highly attractive manner, they always held the conviction that this did not give permission to be sexually harassed at work.

Complicating the problem of domestic violence was heavy abuse of alcohol. Preliminary data collected in these countries indicated a high occurrence of alcoholism that contributed to what the Russians called "family violence," or *nassiliasemya*. The wide abuse of alcohol was seen as the primary cause of domestic violence.

This differed strongly from the western understanding that domestic violence was centered on issues of power and control in relationships. One partner, typically the man, would exert mental, emotional, physical and sexual abuse to control their partner. The western understanding recognized that alcohol exacerbates the problem but is not the underlying cause.

After identifying the problems to be addressed by the work in our grant and establishing baseline data, the next step was the recruitment of trainers. In the beginning, I felt confident that I understood the dynamics of domestic violence and believed that I could be a trainer myself.

I identified and located a police trainer, Bill Baker, at a police chief's meeting in Massachusetts. He was a thoughtful police chief and attorney who was a strong advocate of preventing domestic violence. In time, he would go on to become the Director of Public Safety for Massachusetts and hold many prominent police leadership positions throughout his career. Next, I asked a local emergency room nurse, Paula Lanson, who was also a good friend and the wife of a fellow police officer with whom I had worked. Paula was the ideal example of a nurse that I had identified in the grant that we had written for Gardner. She was smart, temperate, worked closely with police and had a deep understanding of human behavior and the dynamics of domestic violence, having been a victim herself earlier in life.

I soon identified a local family psychologist and therapist to work and train his colleagues in the former Soviet Union. To represent the legal profession, I was able to identify a local district court judge with Eastern European roots who enthusiastically signed on to be our legal trainer. And our women's advocate trainer who had trained Bill Baker was Carole Sousa. Bill highly recommended her to work with women and non-profits. The first team was complete.

The next step was to bring the group together for an orientation. This meeting would focus on giving our trainers a briefing on the current state of affairs regarding domestic violence in Russia, and the cultural differences they would experience, not only in their work but in their living space and society in general. Each member of the team was also given an opportunity to practice their presentations, meet their colleagues and learn from each other. These orientations were critical to forming a cohesive team and presenting a consistent message to their audiences.

For our first trip to Russia for the Domestic Violence Community Partnership Program, we went to the Karelian city of Petrozavodsk, the same city where we began our law enforcement exchange program in 1994. Project Harmony had continued to work in this city for many years, so our office there was well established. We had a talented English speaking Russian manager named Elena Kalyan. Elena would be essential in explaining our program to various constituents that we had contacted to participate in our training. She also had the added gifts of being an exceptional host to our American participants and a first-class interpreter.

Deferring to Elena's experience and wisdom, I asked her once how the American program on domestic violence was received by Russian people and organizations. She said that Russia had a long history of importing thoughts and ideas from the west, dating back to the days of Peter the Great and the building of the beautiful, western style city of St. Petersburg.

Elena's explanation served to deepen my experience of this lovely city with its summer palaces and Hermitage Museum that rivaled Versailles and the Louvre in Paris, France. We would go on to establish three programs in the Russian cities of Petrozavodsk, Volgograd, and Irkutsk, Siberia. The programs were well received in all locations. One outcome of the program was the funding and production of a Russian documentary called "Family Matters." This film was produced and created by a Russian police officer who participated in our first law enforcement exchange. The film went on to win an international award in Russia.

Our time in Siberia proved to be interesting and quite memorable. We were working in Irkutsk and staying with the people and professionals in this part of Russia. This city was open and welcoming to our program and we were freely allowed to address many different audiences that included the police, the Siberian Law Institute, and many local NGOs. When I inquired about the immediate acceptance of our training program and how it had been so enthusiastically received, I was reminded by my Russian colleague that Siberia had historically been a place where people had been banished during the oppressive Soviet times, particularly intellectuals. In reality, rather than suppressing ideas, the practice of banishment helped to establish a region that was known for its independence and free thinking.

Many evaluation processes were put in place during the three years of this program. Coalitions and resource centers for domestic violence were established from Siberia to the Black Sea, notably in locations like Odessa, Ukraine. These programs were most effective in bringing information to women who lived in countries that had been a part of the former Soviet Union. The highest value of this program is in prevention. Like all other work with reform and policing, education and prevention yield the greatest effectiveness to stop and end domestic violence. One particular outcome of these programs served to educate me at a deeper level on what domestic violence is and how the trauma from its effects is present in so many victims and their families.

I thought I knew a lot about the problem, but it was not until I worked with many of the female trainers that we brought over to present that I really began to understand the depth of damage done by this dynamic. Many of the trainers themselves were former victims. Continuously listening to their stories about how they survived their trauma brought a much broader sense of the damage done by domestic violence and the importance of bringing information and assistance to others who were and are trapped in this horrible situation. After listening to our courageous trainers, I stood up one day and shared my experience growing up in a home where I lived and witnessed domestic violence.

I had been in the process of sharing my story with women in Volgograd and I told them that my father had been a World War II veteran and prisoner of war, and that he had come back from the war full of untreated trauma. That unresolved trauma had resulted in his anger and trauma being inflicted on his wife and family. When I finished sharing, a Russian women stood up and told me that my story was very common in Volgograd. It hit me that what I had experienced growing up was widely shared by people from this war-torn city. This realization left me with a feeling of how much people who live in different parts of the world and in different cultures can share the same pain.

Working in this program for nearly three years created great opportunities and privileges to bring this much needed information to countries of the former Soviet Union. I felt it was a resounding success but also felt that it was time to leave. The constant travel schedule of long flights and Russian trains had taken its toll on me and my family. I would return from the trips in constant need of rest and recuperation. I needed to spend time with my family on a regular basis and it was time for new leadership.

At the time, I was working with our program manager, Aimee Thompson, my specialist trainer from Boston Children's Hospital who worked with children who had witnessed domestic violence. She was tapped to replace me as director of DVCPP and lead the program. Even though I had felt very comfortable being the director of this program, it was time for a skilled woman to take the reins.

On September 11, 2001, I was standing in the doorway of Aimee's apartment in Dorchester, Massachusetts. I was meeting with her to go over our programming and transfer the rest of my responsibilities to her new role. Aimee opened the door when I knocked, and in a barely audible tone said, "There's been a terrorist attack."

Her words did not register in my mind, but I sensed that something was very wrong. She invited me inside and we sat and watched live news coverage of the World Trade Center attack. The first plane had already hit one of the towers before I arrived. As we watched live television, we saw the moment that the second plane hit the second tower.

We were both rendered speechless as we watched in stunned disbelief. I sensed strongly that I needed to leave and be with my family 45 miles away in Fitchburg. I told Aimee that I had to go right away. She understood, and I immediately left. I drove home as fast as I could. When I arrived, my boss and friend, Charlie, was at my house as he had planned to meet with me. He had driven 200 miles from Waitsfield, Vermont.

I walked into the house, hugged my wife, and Charlie wrapped his arms around both of us. The mourning and processing of this event was just beginning. It would take me years before all the meaning of that day and its implications would finally set in and eventually contribute to police reform.

Chapter 10

Return to Fitchburg: Executing the Plan

Returning home to the United States was comforting to my health and allowed for rest. I had the time and energy to assess where I was at, and the opportunity to take a pause to reset my thoughts and goals.

I had watched the local news closely over the last couple of years as the city of Fitchburg was strongly considering moving the position of chief of police out of civil service. This would mean the chief's job would be open to qualified candidates from outside the department. The possibility of returning to my first and hometown police department was enticing for many reasons. I knew the personnel at Fitchburg Police, and I could navigate the city with ease. I was certain that my time as chief in Gardner, my education, and my international leadership experience would bring about a sense of service, vision, and a new beginning to this department.

In the interim, I had rejoined the board of Battered Women's Resources (BWRI), our local and regional advocacy agency that served women who suffered from domestic abuse. Besides running educational programs in schools and the community and advocating for protection of women in the court system, BWRI also ran a safe house shelter that served women who were leaving their abusers and were in the process of starting new lives. I had been a board member since my days in Gardner and was now able to recommit my time to the organization as I was no longer traveling.

To my surprise, I was soon offered the position of Interim Executive Director of the agency as the current director had just left to take another job. I was flattered to be offered this leadership post as I was passionate about preventing domestic violence. The work would directly serve the community that I lived in. After three years of directing a complex program like DVCPP, I felt confident that I could handle the position. It was a win for me and the agency. I had the time and skills to do the job, and it afforded the agency a smooth transition period while they worked to hire a full-time executive director.

I found BWRI to be a terrific agency full of talented, dedicated people who played a vital role for the communities in the area. Employing steady and supportive leaders became my most important task. In some ways, being a former police chief opened doors that a person from outside the police world could not open. I could get access to information that was normally not available to non-police personnel. I also learned that a major part of my role as executive director was to oversee the annual fundraiser for the agency. It was a lot of work, but the people in our community came through and we raised a record amount of money during the 10 months I was there.

    While I was doing my best to be a good steward for the agency, I was asked to take the position full time. Although it was an honor to be offered this position, one thing became very clear to me over the months I had spent at the agency: the executive director position at this agency specifically must be filled by a woman. BWRI not only worked to protect abused women in our community but in many ways empowered women to survive, heal, and move forward in their lives. The executive director position needed to be a woman who could lead and empower other women.

    As I continued to monitor the Fitchburg police chief hiring situation, the current mayor made the decision to keep the chief's position under civil service but to open it up statewide to candidates outside the department. The selection process would still utilize the state civil service exam scores, with only the highest scorers considered for the position. The city requested that the statewide test be offered. Given this chance to take the test, I committed myself to the study time required to score as high as possible on the exam.

    Preparing for the exam involved hundreds of hours of studying the recommended books on policing, taking prep courses, and a fierce desire and discipline to pass the test. Rumors of this testing process began when I was still working for Project Harmony. I would take my books to Russia and study when the opportunities allowed. I have a vivid memory of studying on an overnight Russian train traveling from Moscow to Irkutsk, Siberia. I was lying down and travelling in a poorly lit four passenger sleeping coupe. Using a flashlight to illuminate the pages of text, I did my best to focus while trying to ignore the noisy, intoxicated, snoring man sleeping across from me as the train rumbled across the tracks toward my destination.

I would be in Siberia for two weeks working, wearing the very same clothes daily because my luggage had been lost and did not arrive until the end of my time there. I would wash out my underwear each night and dry it on the radiator before going to bed at my host's apartment, eventually falling asleep reading and studying the exam books.

The day finally came to take the test. Like all civil service exams that I had taken previously, it was held at a local public school and monitored by state proctors. I drove to Worcester, Massachusetts, with a friend from the Fitchburg Police Department, Lt. Paul Bozicas, my colleague and lifelong friend who was also taking the exam. He picked me up, and even though he was a friend and former co-worker, he jokingly wished that I was not taking the exam as I was unwanted competition.

Within a month, the scores were released, and among the candidates who had taken the exam from the Fitchburg, my score of 90 out of 100 was the highest of all. No one else had even come close. I felt a strong sense of accomplishment, having done the best I possibly could, and I expected to be considered for the position.

It was not long before disappointment would set in. The mayor's office announced that several other people in the state scored higher. Anyone could take the test, regardless of rank. Also, veterans who took the test and got a passing score of 70 went ahead of non-veterans regardless of their scores. This outcome only served to highlight the absurdity of the civil service testing process as a means to identify and select qualified candidates. Despite this highly flawed system, I felt strongly that if the mayor's office screened the eligible candidates, I could still be chosen for the position. Instead, nothing happened.

When I asked why I was not considered or selected, the mayor replied, "If only you lived in Fitchburg."

This answer made no sense to me as I was from Fitchburg and could easily move back to the city from the nearby town of Westminster where I had lived for the past three years. I had played by the rules, put forth a strong sincere effort, and was still denied the opportunity because I did not live in Fitchburg at the time. I was incensed to say the least. I never understood this logic but had no choice but to accept this decision. It would be later before I began to understand the complex, behind the scenes political games that had led to my exclusion.

Things remained status quo until a new mayor was elected a couple of months later. The new mayor was determined to take the chief's position out of civil service and moved fast with a petition to the state legislature to make this change. Success at the state level meant that things began to move quickly, and soon led to a public announcement that the city was seeking applications for the chief's position from any qualified candidates who wished to apply.

The job was advertised nationally. The mayor appointed a search committee that represented different interests and constituencies to screen and interview candidates to recommend to him for appointment. Having several weeks to prepare for the process, I put together an intentional plan to become the next chief of police in Fitchburg.

My driving question for the people with whom I would meet was, "What would you like to see in the next police chief?"

I made a list of a cross section of people from Fitchburg to meet with, the first being the president of a local credit union. I also spoke with an executive at another financial institution in the city who was very impressed with my efforts and offered me advice and assistance moving forward. A well-known and popular city councilor agreed to meet with me, and when I asked him what he wanted to see in a new police chief, he answered, "Wow, no one has ever asked me what I thought."

He was obviously impressed with my efforts and encouraged me to continue to meet with people. Knowing most of the officers within the police department, I arranged to meet with several of them and ask what they were looking for in a new chief. The most common answer I heard was the need to combat the massive drug problem in the city that was driving the violent crime rate. The officers also said that the department needed to join a regional drug task force in order to more effectively address these issues.

I continued meeting with other constituents in the city. Fitchburg had a large Latino population. I reached out to the Spanish Center in the neighboring city of Leominster that served Latinos in both municipalities. Nedi Latimer, the leader of the organization, was a soft spoken, wise woman of the highest integrity. I set up a time to meet with her at her office in Leominster. When I arrived, I noticed a small, well-organized office with an attentive and polite staff.

When I walked into her office, it appeared that Nedi couldn't hide her disbelief and delight that I had taken the time to talk to her. She shared with me the needs of the Latino community, including support for families and children that ranged from nutrition to housing. I listened, and I came away with a feeling that I had enlisted a strong and much-needed advocate for the future, that coming to seek her help and advice was something that had never happened before.

Getting input from the community proved to be an invaluable step in my process. I felt confident that I was building a strong consensus of opinions from the community. Fitchburg was suffering from a high crime rate and people wanted to see an active effort to combat drug dealing, violence, prostitution, homelessness, businesses leaving the city, and sinking property values. The agenda was long and overwhelming for anyone to address as chief. Although I had cut my teeth in Fitchburg as a police officer and went on to be chief in Gardner, I had been out of the direct loop and progress of policing for almost four years. A lot had changed and there was much new information to learn and to catch up on.

Realizing this, I signed up to attend a community policing conference sponsored by the Department of Justice in Washington, DC, to learn about effective strategies being used in crime-plagued cities. This conference offered me the space and opportunity to listen to stories and accomplishments of others. I began to formulate ideas in my mind that would be different and fruitful in addressing the ongoing problems in Fitchburg.

After having attended this contemporary primer on community policing at my own expense and time, I signed up for an assessment center preparation course in Florida to prepare for this process if Fitchburg opted to use it in the hiring and screening of police chief candidates. An assessment center uses a series of exercises involving real life situations that are given to police chief candidates, who are then evaluated on their effective knowledge and decision-making.

Having gone through an assessment center process before, I did not learn very much, but this time I came away with something different. The presenter talked a lot about personal appearance and how many police officers took this for granted. He said that he observed officers wearing the same suits over and over to the point of wearing them out. I was reminded that when interviewing, it is important to wear a quality suit and shirt that fits properly. Since you will be in close contact with people who will be hiring you, little things go a long way, like taking the time to get a manicure. He emphasized that when you interview, it is your time to shine and to make your best possible impression.

By late summer in 2002, I had submitted my resume for consideration by the hiring committee, and a short while later, I was invited to interview. I arrived early at the City Hall council chambers where the candidates were invited. I felt confident in my new suit, haircut, and manicured nails, and I was ready to go. It was also comforting to know that my wife, Sue, was in the chapel of St. Camillus Church praying for the right thing for me at the very same time. As I walked into the chambers, I saw the committee of eight members sitting opposite me in a curved line. I was formally introduced to them by the chairman, Tom Conry, and he explained the interview process. I don't remember many specifics from the interview, but I know that my answers sent the message that I needed the cooperation of the community to succeed.

One question that I do remember well epitomized the interview and it came from the union president of the police department who was serving as a member of the hiring committee. He started out by saying that the police personnel are union-oriented, and that the union believes in strict seniority when it comes to assigning positions within the department. He then asked me how I felt about that. I answered that I thought bidding by seniority for most positions was probably doable but that there were some sensitive assignments where seniority could not always apply, and the most qualified officer would be a better choice.

He then firmly emphasized to me that the union did not agree with my response. I looked the union president straight in the eyes, and I started my reply, "You have your opinion of what you want, and I have said what I would do," and I paused. Then I turned to look at every other committee member individually, and started again, "The real question is what does the rest of the committee want?"

As I looked at each member, I saw a look of relief and affirmation on their faces. I knew that my answer nailed it. The process was about selecting a candidate who would best serve the citizens of Fitchburg, not the union. The interview ended a short while later. I stood up and thanked the committee for their time and questions and was escorted out of the council chambers by the chairman. When we were alone in the lobby he shook my hand, raised his eyebrows and gave me a big smile. It was an unmistakable signal that the committee was blown away by my answers. I felt confident that I had done my best, that I was well received by the committee, and that I would be looking forward to advancing in the selection.

As it turned out, four candidates were selected by the committee and submitted to the mayor to make his final selection. The finalists were two captains, a lieutenant from the Fitchburg Police Department, and me. We all had personal interviews with the mayor. A day after my interview, I received a phone call from the mayor himself. I was standing in my home office in Westminster with my wife by my side. He offered me the chief of police job. Upon hearing him ask the question, I began to burst with pride and accomplishment inside.

I coolly answered that I was honored to be offered the job and I would gladly accept this new challenge. The phone call ended, and I grabbed my wife, pulling her to the floor and rolling around with glee like kids on Christmas morning. All the time and effort had paid off.

CHAPTER 11

Bag Job:
Or Who Stole My Cheese!

"This whole process was nothing but a bag job!" argued the only city councilor to vote against my confirmation as the new police chief. After the mayor offered me the position, a storm of press came out with some local individuals claiming that my appointment was fixed all along and that no one else was even considered for the job. I was absolutely stunned by the reaction of some people who felt slighted in the process. I had never spoken with the mayor once, neither before nor during the whole process, until I was interviewed.

It is easy to understand the disappointment one feels after applying for a job and failing to get it. I had felt the same way after being a finalist for the chief's job in Chelsea, Massachusetts, a few years prior. Yes, I had been disappointed when I did not get the job, but I felt no ill will toward the appointing authority. Every community has the right to make the decision that they feel is best for them. It seemed to me that my selection was seen as tainted, and that individuals who would benefit from the old civil service system felt slighted. Being a bit blindsided by this public reaction, I decided it best to consult with my attorney to speak publicly on my behalf if necessary. He was a well-known defense lawyer of impeccable talents with the ability to speak with authority. He also stood about six foot five inches tall and had a highly recognizable presence; he was the same attorney who had rectified my appointment as a police officer in 1980 when I first joined the Fitchburg Police Department.

    We met the day before my confirmation was scheduled and I expressed concerns that something nefarious or outlandish could happen. After briefing him on the whole situation, he agreed to attend the council meeting where my confirmation would occur and sit in the gallery behind me, ready to respond if his services were needed. He sat and watched the whole proceeding. His presence was unmistakable, and the message was clear: make sure that this proceeding is run fairly or there may be repercussions.

    In my mind, I imagined a cartoon image of a huge, fierce, drooling junkyard dog with a spiked collar on a chain ready to seize any trespassers who would attempt to publicly tarnish my image. Aside from the remarks by the councilor who was not pleased by my appointment and had voted against it, I was confirmed and sworn in that evening. I later thanked my attorney and was pleased that his quiet presence had assured an orderly confirmation, while also sending a strong message that I expected to be treated fairly.

    In retrospect, I was delighted that all the hard work I had put in to become chief had paid off. Putting together a comprehensive plan to meet with my community and listen, making a deliberate effort to hone my policing skills, and bringing a fresh perspective had won the day. It was understandable that some would see it differently. This application and selection process was new to the city, and the past practice of seniority and testing for appointment were no longer in play. I could empathize with applicants who had never experienced a new, open process, and who saw it as foreign and disappointing. Quite frankly, this was understandable.

The next step to taking over the helm was to meet with the three captains who were the superior officers in the department. One of the captains who had been a finalist for chief, Captain Joe Carbone, shook my hand. He would become a great ally in my efforts to move the department forward. He was the same supervisor who had asked me, "Who the fuck are you?" on my first day on the job.

After my initial hazing early in my career, he had become a lifelong mentor for me. He taught me how to work with people, pushed me to improve my skills, rewarded me for my efforts, and demonstrated the humblest of personality when I ended up being his boss. He joked to a friend, "I was his mentor," and I think he had a strong sense of pride in those words.

As evidenced in my retelling of the Christmas murders, my honeymoon in the new job was over in less than two months. Being shocked into the awareness of the reality of the present crime situation, I instinctively knew I had to reach out to the Latino community.

I called a meeting with my command staff and asked the simple question, "Who can we reach out to in the Latino community to begin to address all this violence?"

I waited for an answer but was met only with silence. It was obvious that we, as a police department, did not have any formal ties to the Latino community. The department had been involved in a series of lawsuits filed by a local attorney representing Latino clients. While I was informed that the department had won most of the suits, I realized that, for whatever reason, the police were constantly on the defensive with this community. Any relationship building would have to start from scratch.

Having grown up during the 1960s and 70s, I had witnessed firsthand the social revolution taking place in our country and in my own city. Controversy and protests over the Vietnam War had been a daily occurrence. Many times, those events would turn violent and even result in people being killed. At the same time, the growing civil rights movement led by Martin Luther King, Jr. and other elements of Black society were protesting racism and discrimination that, in some instances, had led to massive disorder and destruction in our cities. In both scenarios, police and military force were employed to suppress ongoing violence which resulted in abuses and tragedies.

Fitchburg was not spared these happenings and experienced its fair share of desperation and violence. One young Black man, Adrian Ford, emerged as a spokesperson for the Black and minority community in Fitchburg. Originally from New York, Adrian demonstrated and sought out peaceful means to suppress violence and attempted to bring understanding and peace to the community as a whole. He reached out to political leaders and even to the police and was instrumental in establishing the first minority coalition. Adrian and his organization, Three

Pyramids, advocated for the rights of minorities and established funding and programs to raise skills and opportunities within the community.

    I reached out to Adrian and asked to meet with him. He graciously accepted my request and before long I was invited to attend a meeting of the minority coalition being held on Martin Luther King Day. Before a crowded room at Three Pyramids, I cordially introduced myself and expressed my desire to work with all members of the community to suppress violence and work together to build safe and healthy neighborhoods in our city. After I spoke, I offered to take questions from the people in attendance.

    One Black man stood out and shouted at me, "Why don't you take the money you're seizing from drug dealers and put it back in our neighborhoods?"

    I was taken off guard, to say the least, as I did not even know the people in the room. I was just beginning to learn the depths of the crime problems, and yet here I was being confronted by someone who was demanding immediate action.

    Initially I had thought this request to be out of order and was immediately supported by Adrian who acknowledged the upset individual but reminded him that this was my first meeting with the coalition. As it would later turn out, this "hothead" was more on the right track than I could have ever imagined. Yes, he was upset, but like many in the community, he was desperate to see a good faith measure from the white community to support people of color. I grew increasingly aware of just how much they had been disadvantaged and systematically excluded. Overall, I felt a mixed reaction from the people I had met with that day. There was definitely some mistrust from the

Black community, but simultaneously, there was also a sense of something different happening.

This was the first time that a police chief had ever attended a community gathering like this in Fitchburg, and I sensed a feeling from some that they should give me a chance.

Drug related crime and violence continued to plague the city. One of my first priorities was to initiate the drug task force that had been suggested by the officers during the community meeting phase of my plan to become chief. Creating this task force would bring in assistance from several area departments. Detectives assigned to the unit would primarily operate out of Fitchburg. This allowed neighboring municipalities to work proactively to keep drugs out of their cities and towns while also adding a more potent and effective offensive against illegal drug dealing in Fitchburg.

Over the next couple of years, drug search warrants would rise exponentially in the city. The only problem was that the overall crime rate would stay the same. In other words, despite a historic and overwhelming effort by the task force, there was no significant decrease in crime. While the productivity of the drug task force had far exceeded my expectations and lifted morale within the police department and among some politicians, this work was not moving us forward.

I began to look at other initiatives that could potentially improve public safety in our community. The city of Boston had a highly successful model to combat violent crime in the Black community and the other communities of color. It was sponsored by an organization called the Ten Point Coalition. This effort emphasized an ecumenical approach to mobilize communities to address crime. One strategy involved Black ministers partnering with police officers to visit families of at-risk youth. The partnership of police and clergy was a powerful expression of trust. The visits would inform the family that their child was at risk of being involved in, or becoming a victim of, violent crime.

On many occasions, parents were not even aware of the extent to which their child or children were at risk and were deeply grateful for being informed. After initial notification by the police and clergy, the family would then be offered assistance to prevent future violence and reintegrate the child back into a safer community lifestyle. This was just a thumbnail of the work being done in Boston. The work was dubbed the "Boston Miracle," as it had drastically reduced the murder rate in the city, especially within communities of color. I was impressed with what I had read and decided to reach out to the Boston Police and the Ten Point Coalition to try to learn from their efforts.

I connected with Dr. Eugene Rivers, a dynamic and principled Black minister who had devoted his career to stop the senseless murders of Black youth killing each other in Boston. He took exceptional risks and actions by speaking out and identifying the lack of male leadership in single parent families. Dr. Rivers believed that the Black community had a responsibility to address these issues. He reached out to the police and formed partnerships with them to broker truces between warring gangs. His efforts were truly remarkable and were modeled in cities throughout the country.

On one trip to Boston, I was invited to a neighborhood meeting that consisted of representatives from the police, clergy, social workers, probation, prosecutors and other community members. The meeting was held once a week with the purpose of discussing troubled youth who had been identified as at risk or in danger of committing crimes. This information was then passed onto the appropriate agency to contact the family and proactively manage the problem. I was impressed by the cooperation displayed at these meetings by the organizations and private citizens in attendance. There was a sincere desire to prevent crime from happening by sharing vital information that previously would have gone unnoticed by others. This also created a sense of trust within the community itself that focused on increasing public safety. Other vital components were also part of the strategy, but by having an up-close look, I was able to verify that what was happening was truly a "Boston Miracle."

Learning about this process was uplifting and I was inspired to bring some of these successful efforts to my home city. I was particularly taken by the partnership between the clergy and the police. Having received an invitation in the past to meet with several white Protestant ministers, I saw this as a possibility to partner with these clergy leaders. My opportunity to enlist their support came sooner than expected. A short while later, I was attending a team meeting in Methuen, Massachusetts, preparing to participate in an upcoming retreat weekend.

While sitting and listening to a teammate practicing a presentation, I felt a nudge at my elbow. I turned to look at the gentleman who had poked me and his eyes guided me to the table in front of us where my cell phone was buzzing in silent mode. I reached down, grabbed the phone and exited the room to answer the call. It was the police station calling to notify me that another murder had taken place in the city. I requested the location where the murder had occurred, then quickly excused myself from the meeting and drove the 45 minutes to Middle Street in Fitchburg.

The street was dark when I arrived except for the bright streetlight that illuminated the crime scene. I got out of my car and met with an officer, quickly noticing a pool of wet blood on the sidewalk. It was a sickening sight. The pandemic of murders just seemed to go on unabated with no relief in sight. A drug infused altercation had ensued earlier and a Latino man had been shot and killed on the sidewalk in front of a senior housing center.

I was already anticipating the impending negative media response that would continue to paint Fitchburg as "Crime Central." But it wasn't these thoughts that worried me the most. While I was standing in the street, I looked up to my right, scanning the 10-floor building of the senior citizens housing facility hovering above the shooting scene. It was then I noticed a window on the fifth floor and the shadow of a woman peeping out of her window at the edge of her drawn shade. I could only imagine the terror and vulnerability that this woman must have been feeling at this time.

Meeting with the concerned ministers the next day, I expressed my frustration with the continued violence and how I felt that there needed to be some type of public expression of grief and an opportunity for healing for the community. I suggested that the group go to the scene of the crime and offer prayers and words of reassurance to the neighbors and residents of the area.

A day later the group showed up, as did the family of the victim. One of the ministers said a prayer and began to speak and almost immediately, two Latina family members of the victim began to cry and wail loudly, stunning my minister friends. It had been the same type of shock I had experienced when witnessing the three women mourning their loved one on Christmas Day. These women were grieving, expressing a suffering that was not fully understood by these clergymen. And this expression, their tears of hopelessness, were a form of pleading, begging for an end to these tragic events.

Our intentions to bring healing to our community and gather public support did not turn out the way we had anticipated. Even more disturbing to me was the feedback I received from some of my department members that I should not have been at the scene. The officers who criticized me believed that because the man who was shot and killed was drug involved that he was not worthy of any sympathy from the chief of police. I understood how they felt but I did not go to memorialize the victim. My presence at the scene was to openly grieve what was happening to my city and try to create a sense of hope for the future. Plainly, it did not work.

CHAPTER 12

Sayra and Systems: Finally, There was Hope!

Continuing to address the violent scourge in the city and battling the alarmist press was a relentless task. Our best attempts to assert control went unnoticed. Our adoption of a data-driven approach on crime mapping and analysis to give a current state of crime was completely overshadowed whenever a random street person was quoted by the newspaper as saying, "I'm moving out of here as soon as possible!" after a crime had been committed. The reoccurrence of crime and the sensationalizing in the local newspaper continued to create a sense of hopelessness and fear among city residents.

     To address the ongoing drug problems in the city, a methadone clinic was opened to serve people addicted to drugs. The program was designed to help individuals to reduce gradually their dependency and return to a healthy lifestyle. Despite the need for these services, the clinic was seen as promoting drug use and there was speculation that it would increase crime in the area it was located.

To dispel the fears of the community, I took it upon myself to visit and inspect the clinic firsthand. I discovered that the majority of patients being treated there were gainfully employed, functioning adults who were being medically assisted to reduce and eliminate their dependency on illegal drugs. As a follow up, I conducted a crime analysis of the area where the clinic was located, and the data conclusively showed that virtually no crime was occurring anywhere near the clinic. It was fear and misunderstanding about the clinic that was driving a negative attitude about this needed service for our own citizens.

To offset this ongoing daily crisis, I started taking night courses at Suffolk University in Boston. I was fortunate that my employment contract had a provision that would pay for any continuing education I sought while I worked as chief. I enrolled in a Certificate of Advanced Graduate Studies (CAGS) in Organizational Development and Change. These courses gave me the double benefit of learning new ideas and strategies to improve our police department as well as the personal satisfaction of being in a positive and reinforcing learning environment.

The courses were very helpful in my work, but it wasn't until I took a course in systems thinking with professor Carol Sharicz that I truly understood the insidious depth of the problems within my city. Systems thinking provided me with a framework to address these issues anew and offered me the hope that there was potential for a new beginning. The concept of systems thinking originated in 1956 when the Systems Dynamic Group was created by professor Jay W.

Forrester at the Sloan School of Management at the Massachusetts Institute of Technology (MIT). It utilizes computer simulations and different graphs and diagrams to illustrate and predict system behavior. Originally, it was designed to diagnose and solve persistent recurring problems in business. It also evolved as a philosophy and practice to diagnose repeated problems in any kind of organization.

I began to theorize that applying a systems thinking approach in Fitchburg could be a unique way to diagnose, apply resources properly, and finally to address the underlying causes of crime in our city and region. I never professed to have mastered all the rules and concepts of the systems approach, but I could clearly see that my city was caught up in trying to bring "quick fixes" to deep seated problems. The war on drugs relied on the use of overwhelming enforcement tactics such as zero tolerance and arrests to suppress crime. In reality, all that did was to displace crime, increase incarceration rates, and, in many cases, actually increase crime and deepen resentment in the minority community.

In systems thinking language, that is an archetype called "fixes that fail." We were only addressing the symptoms of the problems. If the police department executed a search warrant on a drug dealing house that was causing havoc in a neighborhood, the drug dealers would be arrested and brought to court. This would eliminate that particular problem, but inevitably, another drug house would soon appear. We were not addressing the underlying issues, the origination point, or the root cause of the problems. Instead, we continually applied the same solutions and came out with the same outcomes. To paraphrase Albert Einstein, repeating the same process over and over again and expecting a different result was the definition of insanity. Intrigued by this model, I began to create graphs and causal loops in an attempt to understand why crime was happening and why it kept escalating.

It wasn't until I met a brilliant young Latina, Sayra Pinto, that my understanding of the problems in Fitchburg truly came to light. Sayra was an indigenous woman born in Honduras who had immigrated to the United States as a child. She had been recently hired by Mount Wachusett Community College through a grant from the Kellogg Foundation to improve the performance of Latino students in the public school system in Fitchburg and the region. She came from the urban city of Chelsea where she had worked in the community.

Sayra's task through the community college was to support the agency's mission of "disrupting incarceration rates, poverty, and racism by working with young adults, police, and systems at the center of urban violence to address trauma and bring hope and change to a broken system."

Sayra had begun her work by calling on stakeholders like me, to begin building a trusting partnership. I shared with her my frustration with all the violent crime that was prevalent with Latino youth and the inability to reach out for help from this community to address these problems. Sayra shared with me that one of her major goals was to improve the graduation rate of Latino students at Fitchburg High School. Sayra informed me that nearly 40% of Latino students were dropping out and not graduating. It became crystal clear to me that students who were not graduating from high school would naturally seek out memberships in gangs for support and then engage in criminal activity to make money.

Most certainly, the dropout rate of these students was a major feeder system to our crime problem in the city. It became apparent that many of the issues that we addressed and enforced as cops started way before these teenagers were ever arrested. While in the school, many of the students who dropped out were viewed as disruptive and labeled as "failures."

In Massachusetts, when a youth turns sixteen years old, compulsory attendance of school is no longer required. Both students and school administrators knew this metric, and I witnessed, firsthand, how it was used as a leverage point. Visiting the local high school one morning, I pulled up to see a school administrator outside of the building yelling at a Latino student and saying, "Two more weeks until you're sixteen, and you're out of here!" This dysfunctional interaction occurred right before my own two eyes.

Sayra and I discovered through our conversations that we were both systems thinkers. My learning process had begun at Suffolk, and she had been mentored in this field by the two leading practitioners in the country, Peter Senge and Otto Scharmer from the Sloan School of Management at MIT. She had also been working toward root causes analysis and systemic racism all her life.

Sayra's own life was her laboratory. When she had arrived in the U.S. in the 1980s, she had been separated from her family in this war-torn country. In the U.S., she was nurtured by relatives until she moved to Chelsea. It was here that she experienced the systemic exclusion that resulted in the original high school class of 400 graduating only 200. She was among the best, and she went onto Middlebury College but continued her work helping and saving young lives in Chelsea.

The richness and trauma of her experience went very deep. She had come to Fitchburg willing to share her lessons and experience to improve the life and safety of excluded Latino students. We were both excited to find out that we viewed our joint problems in Fitchburg through a systemic lens, and we agreed that we had to address the root causes of these problems before the situations would improve. It was during one of our first conversations when she took the risk to reach out to me that I expressed my exasperation with all the crime and murder going on in the Latino community. I went on about the absence of Latino fathers and how that fact impacted the youth.

It was then that Sayra took the risk to tell me, "You're the one who has all the power, you have all the money, the guns, the ability to control things! What are you doing about it?"

I thought I knew about system failures, but she reminded me of the first lesson in the process. I had to ask myself, "What do I do, consciously or unconsciously, to make the problem worse?" This was a very counterintuitive question for me, but I had to ask it of myself. Her inference was right; we did have control and power that we weren't using properly.

Through our shared goals and philosophy, Sayra also introduced me to the work of another group from MIT called the Society of Organizational Learning (SOL). Sayra and I conferred with SOL and its varied membership which brought us in touch with other systems thinkers. Attending SOL conferences allowed us to polish our skills and develop a strong relationship built on honest listening sessions. I will always be grateful to SOL, Peter Senge, and Otto Scharmer for allowing me to attend conferences to deepen my understanding of systems thinking methodologies. With a foundation of trust between us set, we began to model our relationship in the community to show that we were both willing to cooperate to solve our problems.

Sayra began introducing me to many Latino mothers. These women had grave concerns for their children: would they be safe and successful growing up in Fitchburg? I listened to many mothers who had encountered racist policies in the school system and in the police department. With Sayra's support and guidance, I learned to listen to their concerns and not respond defensively. It was a new experience for me to sit for a period of time, truly absorb the narratives, and really hear what was being said.

Along with gaining the trust and respect of these Latinas, Sayra introduced me to Joanne Fitz, or as she was better known, "Mama Fitz." Sayra had met with Mama Fitz through her work on the minority coalition that she was putting together. Sayra took me to Mama Fitz's doorstep and porch, situated in a troubled neighborhood in the city. As I approached the stairs, I recognized the elder black woman seated in her rocking chair on her porch. I had driven by this address many times in the past and wondered in my mind, "Wow, this woman has a bird's eye view of all the happenings in the neighborhood."

She was a dignified, astute woman who was a very strong influencer especially in the Black community, and in fact, did know all the goings on in the neighborhood and the city. Sayra had created a beautiful and trusted relationship with Ms. Fitz, and by introducing me, Sayra affirmed that I was different and could be trusted. I would go on to have many conversations with Mother Fitz and to be invited to a church of worship that had a strong influence over the Black community.

One particular interaction was both memorable and revealing for me. My drug officers found out, while gathering intelligence in preparation for a drug raid, that a well-known young man was at high risk of being shot or killed by a rival drug dealer. The young man was arrested on a subsequent drug raid and was held in jail until his next court appearance. His mother called me at the station and started shouting into the phone. She was accusing my officers of being racist. Again, I listened and heard her out, sensing the pain and worry in her voice. When the mother stopped, I informed her that her son's life was in grave danger and that jail was the safest place for him to be right now.

I paused, taking a deep inhalation, and told her, "Ma'am, I do not want to see your son get killed."

On the other end of the line, I could hear the mother burst into tears. She began to open up to me, relaying her concerns for her son's safety. She realized that we had the same goal in mind, keeping her son safe, and she saw that she had an ally in me.

While these listening sessions continued, Fitchburg was once again shocked by another Latino shooting in October, 2006. This time it was at a quinceanera, a fifteen-year-old girl's birthday and "coming of age" party. Quinceaneras are a grand celebration put on by Latino families for their daughters. This one was held at Saima Park, a privately owned, beautiful outdoor facility on the northern outskirts of the city. The parties are quite often elaborate and expensive events and are usually by invitation only.

    I learned that many families who put on these events go well beyond their financial means to hold these traditional rites of passage. Two local teenage boys decided to crash the party and were asked to leave. A skirmish ensued and the teens left. Tragically, they came back a short time later, emerging from a wooded area, shooting and killing one young male teen, and injuring four others. It was reported that panic overtook the crowd and parents had run toward the bar and handed their children over it to hide them for their protection. The assailants left and the police arrived on the scene.

    I was called out from home and responded, arriving to see a field of people in a state of shock and grief. I asked one of my Latino officers at the scene what had happened, and he explained the situation. He then turned to me with a look of emotional frustration and said, "Chief, they won't talk to me!"

    I sensed that he felt some responsibility to find out more information because he was Latino. In an attempt to reassure him, I quickly responded, "This has nothing to do with you."

    This was a crime scene. In general, at an active crime scene, people either did not trust the police or were afraid of us. The parents' negative response to the Latino officer was not personal.

    Again, Fitchburg had news of another murder story hitting the local newspaper. One witness at Saima Park stated, "We have all this violence, and the police do nothing about it!"

I was asked by one reporter, "Do you think Quinceaneras should be cancelled?" I had almost anticipated this question, as the Fitchburg quinceanera shooting occurred on the heels of two recent violent quinceanera events in California.

I remember that I used an uncharacteristically sarcastic tone, as I answered him, "Maybe we should cancel Christmas, too?"

Violent events tend to occur around that holiday, as well. As usual, everyone was looking for short term answers after the fact and refused to look deeper into why all this violence was occurring.

On the next day, I met Sayra and we talked about this latest violence. She told me about the sadness in the Latino community and I shared her sense of helplessness. A couple of days later, a wake was held in the evening for the victim who was killed at the party. Again, I felt the need to be present at this event even though I did not know who was responsible for the murder or who the people were.

I chose to go to the funeral home and park across the street to observe from my car the sadness of the people coming and going. At one point. I looked up and saw Sayra walking to the front door of the funeral home. I got out of my car and walked over to her. We embraced as she cried in my arms. I couldn't ease anyone's pain, but I felt that my presence would at least send a signal that I cared and grieved with them.

It was easy for the press and the public to look at a murder like this as a savage act committed by savage people. But underneath it all, other forces were at work. This was an event that had traumatized the Latino community and its students. Yet, Sayra told me that the high school did not even bring in grief counselors to the school. It was more obvious to me that there were two systems in play: one that would serve the white community, and one that excluded the Latinos. Systemic racism existed in our city and school system. It was not intentional discrimination, but a process that systematically provided success for some and failure for others.

Through further discussions with Sayra and the Latino mothers, I began to have a *metanoia*, a change of heart, about how I viewed my own police department. I made it my habit to keep my office door wide open, trying to send the message to all of transparency and availability. One day I was sitting in my office looking out into the small lobby area where the public entered to obtain records, accident reports, and the like. I observed an older Latino man approach the two clerks who were seated there to service the public. It became obvious that the man did not speak English, so one of our clerks pointed to a chair and told him to sit and she would get someone who spoke Spanish to help.

I continued to work and after several minutes saw that man was still waiting. Finally, more time had passed, the lobby door opened, and our bilingual detective began to interpret for the man. The conversation lasted only a minute and the man turned around and left the lobby. I never knew what this man was asking for, but it seemed wrong to me to have a man wait for such a long time only to ask a question and leave right away.

A few minutes later, I was talking to one of my supervisors and mentioned that when one of the clerks who was soon scheduled to retire, we would hire someone who speaks Spanish to better serve our growing population.

"Will that person be qualified?" the supervisor questioned me.

Months earlier, I would not have blinked at this answer but after learning about the exclusion of so many people in our city, what I actually heard was: "Most of them are not qualified so we have to be careful who we hire."

I knew this answer was not intended to discriminate against anyone, but it had become clear to me that by asking these questions, we were just proliferating systemic racism. Later, I told this story to several area police chiefs and officers, and they all responded the same way: "What's wrong with that question?"

In reality, my education by Sayra and the Latino community revealed a blind spot that I never knew existed. This was confirmed a few weeks later at a City Council meeting where I was giving an update on the crime situation in the city. I arranged for Sayra to also speak before the council to share her views and the work of the Latino coalition. She spoke eloquently and truthfully about the state of the Latino community. I was proud and impressed by her presentation.

The next day, I picked up the local newspaper and saw that my comments were quoted in a front-page story. It was glaringly obvious to me was that Sayra and her comments had been completely omitted.

Later in the day, the reporter who had written the story came into my office to ask me questions about ongoing crime issues. I then told him that I was very disappointed that the newspaper had not printed or said anything about what Sayra had reported to the City Council.

Not only was I unhappy about this recent article, but I was frustrated with the ongoing coverage of this paper. I said, "Your newspaper is racist! You did not print one word of the important information that Sayra had said. You discounted it."

It was not long before I received an irate phone call from the editor who vehemently resented my comments to his reporter and denied any taint of racism by his paper. I listened to what he said and told him that I stood by my comments. Apparently, he did not like the fact that I had exposed his blind spot about systemic racism.

Sayra and I continued our conversations and conferencing. About this time, I received a phone call from the editor of the newspaper who asked me if I would be interested in participating in a process to raise funds for some activities for youth in the tri-city region of Fitchburg, Leominster and Gardner during the coming summer. It was at this time that it occurred to me that this could be a great opportunity to do some truly meaningful work that would address the crime problems in the region and address the underlying issues that continued to perpetuate these problems.

CHAPTER 13

Searching for Answers: Unexpected Results

I met with Sayra shortly after I received the call from the newspaper editor and told her of his idea to raise money for summer activities for youth. I suggested putting together a broad section of strategic community members from the region and training them in the methodology of systems thinking. The idea was to invite leadership to participate in a process that would help us to understand why crime was happening in our cities. It would also create an opportunity to share our joint experiences and frustrations on the occurrence of crime and gain a fresh perspective of how we, as a group, could address these issues moving forward. Traditional methods of enforcement were productive but ineffective in preventing and reducing crime.

Sayra was all for it, and we were soon seeking out facilitators to lead this unparalleled effort. Knowing that there would be a cost incurred to put this endeavor into reality, Sayra approached the local community college that was employing her and convinced them to support our work. She asked for funding to pay for the trainers. The president of the college, Dan Asquino, readily complied.

After conceiving this idea, we identified many stakeholders from the tri-city region to participate. Our invitation list included representatives from local law enforcement, including members of the regional drug task force and probation, as well as social workers, educators, hospital personnel and, for the first time ever, a contingent from the Latino community. The number of participants numbered near 40 people. We met and hired Sara Schley and Joe Laur of Seed Systems, experts in systems thinking, to provide the training for our assembled group.

In the beginning of the training, concepts such as mental models were examined. The website for Ecology and Society defines mental models as "personal internal representations of external reality that people use to interact with the world around them. They are constructed by individuals based on their unique life experiences, perceptions and understandings of the world."

All people form mental models to help visualize and make sense of the world around them. Some mental models can be helpful, like when you are visualizing the shortest route to a destination, but others can be inherently biased, prejudicial, and downright damaging. For example, if a person has a mental model that a young Latino man is probably a drug dealer, then that person will likely have a tainted vision of the character and probabilities of Latino men.

Another concept that was examined by our broad cross section of participants was "the tip of the iceberg." While this graphic is more familiar today and is commonly shared on social media platforms to illustrate the complexity of what we see on the surface versus the depth of what's below, this pictorial representation was groundbreaking to our group in 2006. Our trainers projected a graphic showing a small tip of an iceberg protruding from the water, while underneath the water was a mammoth block of ice.

The lesson here, our trainers explained, was that when we see a sign of trouble, we need to be aware that there could be a much more complicated explanation for what we are observing. For instance, a crime is seen as a crime, and a perpetrator should be punished, but if we do not address the conditions that cause or influence the perpetrator to act in that way, we will continue to see others committing the same crime.

After reviewing these concepts, the attendees were broken up into several small groups, each at their own table. Our groups were then given questions by the facilitators, such as "Why is crime occurring in our communities?"

The groups mapped out their responses on paper using causal loops to look at what was causing crime. Next, we worked together to examine the interventions that could potentially stop the cycle of violence. There were many spirited conversations and dozens of causal loops drawn and examined. These two days of focused work and discussions provided members of our group with not only the opportunity to learn about systems thinking but gave them the language to describe causal reactions and the ability to discern the reasons why crime was occurring in our region.

A Latino gentleman was selected to report on his small group's conclusions after the second day of our work. He stood up and identified systemic racism and lack of economic opportunity for at-risk youth as the cause of crime in our cities. Immediately, the publisher of the newspaper, now in attendance, stood up and stated "We are not going to be talking about racism! That was not the point of this effort!"

Both college presidents in attendance stood up and voiced their opinion, agreeing with the newspaper publisher that racism was a non-starter. Sensing the frustration of the people who had worked so hard over the last two days, I moved to respond. I saw two of my police colleagues exchange a look with each other, and then both glanced at me, and I knew immediately what they were thinking: "This is where Eddy is going to lose it! Here it comes!"

I worked hard to stay in check. After two days of amazing work, I was devastated to see this descend into white denial. I was feeling very emotional and sensitive to this public rejection of the group's findings. I felt that I was witnessing firsthand the exclusion that we had been talking about during the process and that Sayra had been telling me about since our very first meeting together. I knew in my head and my heart that this was the very reason that Sayra did the work she did, because white systems of oppression were still at play even within a collaborative, progressive-minded group like ours.

The Latino gentleman was speaking for the segment of our city most ravaged by the scourge of crimes and drug abuse, and right before my eyes, what he had to say was being immediately discounted by the white men in power. How could I not lend my voice to support him? I owed it to him, I owed it to Sayra, and I owed it to myself.

I stood up and in a firm voice announced, "Yup. We are absolutely going to discuss the role of systemic racism and its effects on our crime problem."

It was later that Sayra told me when I spoke up in that meeting, speaking truth to power, it was a pivotal moment for Fitchburg. It was the first time a white leader and police chief had publicly supported the Latino community. I don't think that the newspaper publisher or the college presidents were even conscious of how dismissive they were being towards what this gentleman had said. They, like myself, had been conditioned to see the world and our local problems through the lens of a privileged point of view, and felt no intentional responsibility to talk about such a profound topic impacting our city and country at large.

The expectation for this group working together was to unite local leaders over the common goal of raising money for our youth, but some participants were not prepared to hear why there was such a need to address these severe problems. The meeting ended on this note, and we were tasked to continue our work on dismantling systemic racism in Fitchburg.

At our next meeting, we began our discussion on racism. The group watched the Academy Award winning movie of 2004, "Crash." This movie centered on people exercising tolerance and respect for each other regardless of race, especially during times of crisis. The movie emphasized that all people were the same, and that we all had a strong desire as human beings to be treated equally and honorably. This was one of a number of exercises and discussions to approach racism in a safe, nonjudgmental environment.

There was no identifiable tipping point in these conversations, but progress was evident as people were talking honestly and openly about their feelings, and others listening without arguing. Adding to the success of these conversations was a summer jobs program put together by Sayra and her staff to employ at-risk youth working in the city parks and developing leadership skills at the same time. Jason, a towering, strong young Latino man and ex-gang member who was Sayra's assistant, was able to identify young men who were involved in or vulnerable to gang activity that were well suited for summer work at a crucial time in their lives.

Several of the stakeholders, including the two colleges and the newspaper, agreed to donate funds to employ at-risk youth. I decided that I would contribute significant funding from our drug forfeiture account. This was the money, assets, and properties that had been seized when arresting criminals who committed drug crimes. Massachusetts and federal laws allowed for police departments to use this money for discretionary police spending. Historically, these funds were used to pay for overtime hours worked by members of the drug unit, and to buy equipment for enforcement purposes.

I decided that we would appropriate these funds to pay for summer jobs for at-risk youth. Ideally, these funds would act as a preventative measure, the hope being that gainful employment would reduce the need to engage in unlawful ways of making money. It was a powerful moment when I realized that we were employing the very suggestion that was made to me by the Black gentleman at my first meeting with the

Minority Coalition at Three Pyramids. He urged me to do exactly what I was doing now. He had been more right than I could have ever imagined at the time.

Since I did not need the approval of the mayor or city council to allot this money, I decided to be quiet about how I utilized these funds. It was likely that the rank-and-file officers would have strongly disapproved of this expenditure. This money was seen as "law enforcement money," and I sensed my department would not take kindly to it being used for prevention and intervention instead of for enforcement.

Despite my fears about how this could have been perceived, the summer jobs initiative was fully funded and went forward as anticipated. I watched as the crime rate declined during this usually active, violent season. Just as importantly, it was a demonstrated good faith act by the police department to the Latinos in the city.

Sayra and I continued to model our partnership by appearing on local cable access television to explain our ongoing work. We emphasized that we were no longer interested in quick fixes to suppress crime. We were working together to address the root causes of crime and that it would take time to show results.

My department had led a strong effort to suppress drug dealing in Fitchburg. Our officers and the regional drug task force had previously increased drug search warrants several hundred percent over the last year, and there had been no significant drop in crime. We realized that enforcement alone would not solve our problems and that we had to deal with the underlying reasons for why crime was happening. We could never arrest our way out of this predicament.

We explained our regional systems thinking exercise and how the participants had identified systemic racism and lack of economic opportunity for at-risk youth as the underlying causes of crime, and that we were actively working to address these issues by shifting our strategies and resources. It wasn't until years later that I became aware of the Kerner Commission report. This commission was put together by President Johnson back in 1968 to examine the social unrest exemplified by the rash of violence occurring in Black communities in major American cities. The panel had consisted of moderate social scientists who had done an in-depth study of these problems and concluded that the underlying causes of these problems were systemic racism and poverty, the exact same conclusion that our small local group had identified in their humble but amazing work.

Just as white leadership in our community in 2006 had soundly rejected their findings, President Johnson was reported to have been livid with the findings of his commission in 1968 and had dismissed their findings outright.

Instead, Johnson decided to institute his War on Poverty that was supposed to raise people out of hardship but instead had the unintended effect of institutionalizing it through programs like expanding low-income housing and welfare benefits. Johnson, like the leadership during our local work, did not want to do the hard work of participating in discussions and listening and responding to people who were victims of a society built on systemic racism.

Having a new understanding of the underlying conditions that spawned the occurrence of crime in our area, I met with members of my command staff, asking them for ideas on how we could move forward to address crime. Two of the supervisors wanted to see the formation of a team to address gangs and violence. I listened to their ideas, then instituted a new unit named the STRAIT (Strategic Tactical Response and Intervention) Team. The mission of STRAIT was to identify neighborhood hotspots and utilize creative approaches to address ongoing violence. Along with these tasks, the team was responsible for building relationships with the youth in these areas.

  The mission of STRAIT brought the much-needed element of enforcement to address safety in the city but also added the long term and more effective components of prevention, intervention, and creating trust within these troubled places. STRAIT organized activities like attending Celtics and Red Sox games with neighborhood youth supported by funding from local merchants and personal donations. These trips allowed our officers to mix and interact with kids from diverse neighborhoods in a positive and friendly manner, providing an opportunity for officers and kids to get to know each other rather than meeting only in times of crisis.

  I attended both of these events. Many kids attended, along with adults and parents. At the end of the Celtics game, we were in the process of dropping off people by bus in one of the neighborhoods when a Black man said to me, "Thank you, Chief. That was really nice of your officers."

  I was taken aback by this remark but realized that this man was expressing sincere gratitude to our police department for doing something positive for them. I also realized that an event that I saw as a common occurrence in my world was a very special experience for kids and folks who had never seen the inside of the new Boston Garden. This was another example of exclusion that many people of color were not usually able to participate in because of the effects of systemic racism and poverty.

Another positive effort to connect with our disadvantaged youth was the creation of a Police Athletic League (PAL) program. One of my officers, Dave Gordon, who worked closely with youth basketball leagues, asked me to institute this program that would partner police with kids. The program centered around working in athletic settings to prevent kids from getting into trouble, mentor them in life skills, and promote good behavior and citizenship, key elements for success in life.

Dave Gordon asked me to attend a national convention for PAL that would provide direction on how to put a program together. There had been ample evidence of the positive effect of this popular program in countless cities throughout the country. I approved his request. He told me that a civilian community member would have to accompany him to the training. When he told me the name of the individual he wanted to take with him to the training, I learned that it was a man that I had encountered during my younger years on the force. He had been troubled at the time, coming from tragic circumstances, and was now a grown adult who wanted to give back. He was a perfect example of the kind of youth that we needed to impact with the PAL program.

PAL was eventually formed and did much good work in our city, bringing us closer to our young people and their needs. I was proud of the officers that had started and participated in this program. Around this time I instituted a management change by creating the position of a public information officer. This new position was vital to getting my message across to my city and police department. I needed this ally to amplify what we were doing in our city to implement the much-needed change in our approach to addressing crime. The sergeant I had in mind for this position, Glenn Fossa, was bright and thoughtful. He was a natural at talking to people and he had great potential to represent our department. He would also manage the unrelenting assault by the press who were always looking to talk to me.

    I sent Sergeant Fossa out west to be trained as my new public information officer and he took on the role with great zeal, devotion and loyalty to the police department and myself. He was a round peg in a round hole who was being utilized to his full potential. At the same time, he was personally fulfilled and grateful for the opportunity. On the first day Glenn took over the job, the department experienced a serious crime involving drug dealers breaking into a house, kidnapping a young woman, sexually assaulting her and leaving the city with the victim. This incident triggered the first Amber Alert from the Fitchburg Police. The Amber Alert was a new state program that alerted major news coverage of a missing person in danger.

    The media response was overwhelming. It included television trucks and reporters from Boston and as far away as New York. Glenn came to me since this was all unfolding on his first day and I simply told him, "Don't worry, just do your job." He would later relate to me how grateful he was for my patience and understanding in supporting him in this immediate crisis. He became a key ally and spokesperson for me and the next two chiefs in Fitchburg. Glenn still works to this day with our local FATV station serving our city, even in retirement.

As much as we were making progress on several fronts partnering with our citizens, crime and the circumstances it created still existed. Like the issue of the methadone clinic, there was a major concern about the establishment of a needle exchange program for drug addicts. The service center was located just off lower Main Street. Our city had been identified by the Massachusetts Department of Public Health as having a significant heroin problem. The purpose of this program was to stop the spread of AIDS by ensuring addicts use clean needles to slow the transmission of this fatal disease.

As soon as the place opened, it was seen by many in the community as attracting drug addicts, promoting drug use and crime, and was yet another blight that hurt the image of the city. The department soon got a credible report that two known criminals planned a house break when they met up at the needle exchange program. To get an accurate picture of what this needle exchange program did, I made a visit to the center. I was met by the manager of the program who strongly resisted my concerns of what was going on at the center. It turned out that the initiation and management of this program was overseen by gay white men who sincerely wanted to stop the epidemic of AIDS in our city and state. In reality, they had no experience dealing with a drug addicted, criminal element and the behavior that they manifested. I advised them to hire security. They complied, and the program continued without any more serious problems.

These stories all illustrate crime and its effects as symptoms of deeper problems that are interdependent on each other. In all cases, looking for quick fixes only temporarily solves problems that will then inevitably return. It was only when we looked at and addressed the underlying issues fostering crime that the problems in Fitchburg finally changed in the city. It did not happen overnight. There were no immediate results, but instead, a steady process of listening and empowerment. For these efforts I am proud to say I received the Individual Achievement in Civil Rights Award from the International Chiefs of Police in 2011.

Chapter 14

In the Shadows: Negotiating the Pain

Social media was not around when I was involved in local policing, at least not in the capacity that it is today. I look back on that now with gratitude. While the internet is a powerful tool for seeking information, there also exist deep troves of misinformation. Social media would have been a different front for fighting battles that I did not need while being chief of police in Fitchburg.

In recent years, I have fallen into the same trap as others, creating rancor and bitterness with some of the posts I have authored or shared on social media, even alienating some of my closest friends. It was hard to avoid that as I watched people become further divided over the handling and politicization of the Coronavirus pandemic, the election of 2020, and the racial tensions that flared over the summer of 2020.

My heart sank with the senseless murders of Breonna Taylor and Ahmaud Arbery, but I could hold my tongue no longer when George Floyd died at the hands of a police officer on May 25, 2020, in Minneapolis, Minnesota. Having called for police reform throughout nearly my entire career in law enforcement, I thought that now, more than at any previous time, my experiences in Gardner and Fitchburg would resonate and could help bring about change in these cities.

I reminded my friends on social media that Fitchburg had faced a similar situation as Minneapolis with the shooting death of a young, unarmed Black man while I had been chief. Some were quick to point out that justice was not truly served to the victim or to his family in how the case was handled. As people organized last summer and held peaceful protests in Fitchburg and the neighboring cities of Leominster, Gardner, and Worcester, and even in suburbs like Ayer, Bolton, and Harvard, I was transported back to a cold fall day in 2005.

Fifteen years earlier, my unmarked Ford Taurus had rolled along Main Street as dusk was just beginning to fall. My eyes scoured inconspicuous places where I could park to observe the moving memorial which was slated to make its way to the Upper Common. A peaceful march had been organized to begin at Moran Square, a historic district at the lower end of Main Street, and would proceed up the entire length, ending at the public gazebo. The department was on high alert, ready to act if any disorder was suspected to happen.

Our street supervisor had met with the leaders of the march before it began and told them that the police supported, and even encouraged, their right to march and the desire to express themselves. At the same time, organizers were openly warned by the department that violence was not only discouraged but would not be tolerated. A heavy police presence at the start of the march underscored this sentiment.

As the march proceeded, I parked my car out of sight, but I was still able to keep my eyes on the action. Nearly 40 people were part of the somber procession, and I noticed the flickering of candles held by some in the group. They moved along, almost as if they were floating down the street, until they arrived at the gazebo in the Upper Common without any incidents. In an orderly yet quiet manner several people took turns speaking. I don't remember much about what was said, but I do remember hearing the pain in their voices. I felt empty and helpless to do anything about it. There was one definite positive outcome. As promised by the organizers, at no time during the march or the rally that followed did the protest result in any kind of violence.

A few nights prior, in the very early hours of November 3, 2005, I had received an alarming call from the department. A 19-year-old black man had been shot dead by a Massachusetts state trooper in the city after having been involved in a car chase. The sergeant on the desk did not have all the details yet but wanted me to be aware. I thanked him for the call, but any attempt at restful sleep at that point was futile. After tossing and turning for what seemed like hours, I got myself out of bed and tried to prepare for the day that lay ahead of me.

By this time in my career, I was no longer the new kid on the block, doubting myself or second guessing my decisions as I had done on Christmas in 2002. My gut and my heart had always told me that people should come first, that forging connections and relationships was what we were designed to do biologically as human beings. But police work was not a field where this viewpoint was traditionally welcomed.

However, by 2005, I had gone beyond the charge given to me by the sitting mayor, to fight the war on drugs and crime, and I had made inroads with community leaders and organizers. I saw the growth in my department and in myself as I developed an awareness of the collective pain and trauma that our minority community was experiencing. Our newspapers had vilified different racial groups, pointing to the problems with crime and drugs. I did not have all the details about the shooting in my city that had happened just hours before, but I knew that I could not allow the media to oversimplify or sensationalize this tragedy. This should not be what was putting Fitchburg on the map.

I braced myself for the day ahead, drawing on the lessons of my sobriety to take one minute, one hour, one day at a time. I opened my office door, turned on the lights, and before I was even seated, the phone rang with a demanding and unforgiving tone. I answered it with my standard greeting, "This is Chief Cronin. How can I help you?"

Before the words were even out of my mouth, I heard the direct voice of black community leader and clergy member Tom Hughes. "What happened, Chief?"

In that intense and sad moment, we had both dismissed the formality of greetings. I knew Tom to be a man of honor and integrity in the community. He deserved a direct and honest response from me. I started by telling him what I knew to that point.

By that time of the morning, I had already been briefed by the sergeant in charge. I decided that it was time to tell Tom what I could. I explained that during the overnight hours, a young Black man named Preston Johnson was being pursued by the state police. Mr. Johnson was known to both our local officers and the state police for prior convictions.

What might have been a routine traffic stop resulted in a car chase due to Mr. Johnson's refusal to stop his vehicle. As the pursuit headed into Fitchburg, our police were notified and asked to assist the state police. As the young man drove his car onto a side street, he was eventually stopped and partially blocked by a Fitchburg officer and his car. I felt the need to mention to Tom that the Fitchburg police officer involved was Black. Immediately identifying my officer as Black was an attempt to show Tom that my officer's response was not racially motivated.

I then explained to Tom that after my officer's car had blocked the path of Mr. Johnson's vehicle, the young man had accelerated towards my officer. At this point, the state trooper had arrived at the scene, pulling his cruiser behind Mr. Johnson's vehicle. The trooper continued to yell lawful orders for Mr. Johnson to stop his vehicle. Mr. Johnson did not listen, and from the state police officer's vantage point, he saw the young man's vehicle advance towards my officer. Believing my officer to be in grave danger, the state police officer jumped out of his car and discharged his sidearm, striking Mr. Johnson. The young man was dead at the scene.

There was a pause on the other end of the line. Taking a breath, Tom then said, "Chief, if you say it happened that way, I believe it." I felt honored that Tom had taken my word and accepted the facts as I knew them. The phone call ended, and I hung up. The call with Tom had been a difficult conversation. It had helped me to prepare for the dozens of calls I would be getting throughout the course of the day, namely the onslaught of news outlets wanting my comments on the event. I survived my first challenge of the day.

While I did not know it at the time of my call with Tom, I subsequently learned that my Fitchburg officer believed that he was going to be struck by Mr. Johnson's vehicle. The officer revealed that had the state trooper not acted, my officer would have fired his own weapon in self-defense. This information, combined with the trooper's assessment and reasoning for discharging his firearm have always been prima facie evidence that these officers acted legally and justly on that terrible evening.

While speaking with Tom, I could have been more formal. I could have responded to his question in an official capacity, speaking to him the way I would a local reporter. I could have placated him and dodged his question, saying that the state police and the District Attorney's office were in charge and that I was not allowed to comment. But that was not the type of police chief my community needed, and Tom was entitled to a better answer than "No comment." The residents of Fitchburg deserved better. It was obvious to me that creating trust in the community, especially with minority members, was paramount to any protocol. I had worked hard to develop relationships that were meaningful, to gain the trust of my residents, and now was not the time to stonewall them and hide behind bureaucracy.

While I had told Tom everything I knew at the time of our call, I had failed to mention that this was not a Fitchburg police investigation. The shooting had involved a state police officer and thus, we had no legal jurisdiction in the investigation. The determination of facts in this case was up to the state police. Notwithstanding legal jurisdiction over the shooting, Fitchburg was still my city. I saw it as my responsibility to help begin the healing process.

One of the first lessons I learned that had shaped my leadership style was from Steven Covey's book, *The Seven Habits of Highly Effective Leaders.* Covey advised leaders, "Seek first to understand, then to be understood." Since the time of the Christmas murders of 2002, I had sought to understand the issues in Fitchburg, and I had done that through connecting with people, spending countless hours engaging with and listening to members of the minority community. I had invested much of my time each day identifying key community leaders and had made listening to their experiences a priority.

It was now time to withdraw from what Covey called the "emotional bank account" that I had built up through trust and honesty with these individuals over the last three years. I knew at that moment what my next step would be. Later in the day, I drove to the Three Pyramids, a community development corporation in Fitchburg. It was led by executive director Adrian Ford, a Black civil rights leader in our city whom I had come to know quite well. Twenty years after opening the Fitchburg chapter of Three Pyramids, he had founded the North Central Massachusetts Minority Coalition, a multicultural group dedicated to racial, gender, and economic equity in the region. Mr. Ford had a long history of dealing with racial strife in the city going back to 1969. He was a constant in the ebb and flow of race relations in Fitchburg over the past three decades.

My internal compass was telling me that Adrian was the person with whom I needed to speak. Adrian had seen the good, the bad and the ugly of race relations in our community. Many times, he had been maligned by some in the area for his actions and stands, but I saw a man who had withstood the test of time and had given his all to a cause he held dear to his heart. Adrian was a survivor of turbulent times and had successfully persevered regardless of the challenges.

When I pulled up in my unmarked car, Adrian was standing outside Three Pyramids. I needed his key insights into how the minority community would feel and respond to this recent tragic event. After I caught his eye, Adrian strode over to my vehicle, opened the door, and folded himself into the passenger seat. With a silent glance, I felt his appreciation for my being there, and he knew instantly that I needed his support and counsel.

"What's up, Chief?" he offered, with an empathy in his voice that I never forgot. I was lucky to have Adrian as an ally. Part of me wanted to discuss logistics, how we could go about tempering the reaction of the community to this senseless death. But this was not the time for strategizing. We were two men who were grieving the death of a 19-year-old. As we talked this through, I also sensed that we had a shared interest in preventing this situation from devolving into more violence.

Two days later, the march and rally were held peacefully to honor the memory of Preston Johnson. Certain of the criticism I would face from my fellow law enforcement colleagues, I talked myself out of actively participating in these events. I didn't want my involvement to appear as though I was protesting the police action that led to the shooting. But at the same time, I wanted to be counted among those in Fitchburg who genuinely felt the loss of a young man whose life was wasted on this most unfortunate experience. In a sense, everyone aware of the shooting death of Preston Johnson shared feelings of upset and hurt. But unlike so many other places in the United States, it seemed that this incident would pass without any additional violence.

I had to ask myself why it was that Fitchburg was able to withstand the strain of this incident when other communities would explode from the racial tension. Adrian provided some answers. After this tragedy occurred, Adrian wrote a compelling analysis in an op-ed he penned for the local newspaper. He was bold and uncompromising in demanding restraint from all members of the community, and he advised not to rush to judgment about what had happened. Regardless of the outcome of this investigation, he wisely wrote that some white residents felt fear and resentment towards minority communities and how some whites misunderstood Black youth. Adrian wrote about the long-standing systemic racism that had kept minorities in poverty and had excluded them from having fair chances in society and life.

I was beginning to truly understand this resentment and it is no wonder that a tragic incident like this would anger so many people. Another concern that Adrian highlighted was the lack of response from white community leadership in expressing their sadness over the loss of life of this young man. By all accounts, it looked as though Preston Johnson had learned from his previous convictions and had been trying to turn his life around.

There was another side of Preston, and there was more to his story besides the recent events that had led to his tragic death. Adrian did write that the police department had been an exception to the silence from traditional white leadership, crediting both me and the Fitchburg officers for making inroads into the minority communities. He noted how the police were actively reaching out to minority youth to improve trust and to develop relationships. We had several initiatives like our STRAIT team, whose mission was twofold: to combat the occurrence of violence and drugs sweeping the city and to work with at-risk youth as mentors to create trust and to steer them away from drugs and violence.

Adrian's endorsement of our department was a further impetus for me to be as transparent and understanding as possible with the array of intense feelings held in the community. In a later conversation with Adrian, I shared with him that I felt like I had to stay in the shadows sometimes, like on the night of the protest. I felt that I could not publicly express how I felt for fear of the anger and retribution that would be directed towards me.

I realized that Adrian was in the same position as me. He was a spokesperson and representative to the minority community, and while he empathized with the feelings members held, he refused to feed the anger or encourage violence. Adrian sought truth and justice, and listened to his constituency, but did so with the wisdom and balance of a man who had suffered and survived through many years of trying to bring about change. He had my deepest respect.

Chapter 15

A Virus Takes Leave:
Back to the International Arena

When I look back on all the work that we did in Fitchburg in 2005 to address crime and systemic racism, I am pleased with what we accomplished. When I started as chief, the murder rate was higher per capita than the city of Boston and we had a Latino dropout rate in high school of 40%. Thanks to the changes that were put in place during my tenure and continued by police and political leadership thereafter resulted in *one murder* in the city in 2021 and a dropout rate for Latinos that was *less than 8%*. Those improvements indicate to me that the work we did was ahead of our time.

Since the murder of George Floyd and other similar crises in our country, the white community is beginning to acknowledge the presence of systemic racism as the underlying reason for the existence of such wide disparity in our country. This awareness has occurred only in recent years.

Particularly because of all of the improvements we made in Fitchburg, I wish that my time spent there had ended on a more positive note, but it was not to be so. In 2007, Fitchburg experienced a catastrophic financial crisis that resulted in mass layoffs throughout the city and the police department. At about that time, we submitted our annual budget. The City Council responded by slashing our requests due to the large shortfall.

What was shocking to me was the manner in which they did it. I expected that the results would be dire, but I never expected the way the budget would be slashed. The council chose to layoff my entire communications and dispatch staff that consisted mostly of women. The union had pressed the council to lay off the civilian dispatchers because they were not uniformed officers. There was no effort to save even a few of the jobs of these women. This action was, to me, antithetical to everything that I had promoted as a police chief over the last five years.

Everything I had learned and tried to do was based on empowerment. To me, these women were being treated as second-class employees, and this move protected the positions of police officers but did not best serve the interests of the people of Fitchburg. For years, the department administrators had strived to professionalize the communications section of our police department. Police officers had been poorly utilized in the role of civilian dispatchers and had historically avoided it at all costs.

It was tough to see police officers laid off but sacrificing services to the city was not the answer. This decision by the City Council made my position as chief of police untenable. I had dedicated my time to do things the right way and the fair way to all concerned. Attempting to bring modern policing and management to the police department had been derailed in a crisis by local and union politics at the expense of female employees and the citizens of Fitchburg.

I asked for and received a buyout of my contract from the mayor and ended my time at the Fitchburg Police Department. It was not the ending I had intended. There was no fanfare, no thanks, but only political disdain from a police union that felt aggrieved by my decisions. and the local newspaper that decried the city buying out my contract.

Despite the ongoing and ensuing acrimony tainting my departure, I would not change one thing and would make the same choices if I had to do it over again. It wasn't until later, during a conversation with my dear friends Sayra Pinto and Professor Otto Scharmer from the MIT that I began to make sense of my demise in Fitchburg.

Otto listened to my story and said to me, "Ed, you were a virus to the system. When a virus enters a system, the antibodies all combine and attack to kill the virus."

That statement was another reminder that the work that we had done was groundbreaking and effective, but when the boundaries are perceived as crossing elements of that status quo, these forces can and will come together to eliminate you, even to their own detriment.

As a fifty-four-year-old out of work ex-police chief, I felt very uncertain about my future. My wife and I had always been fiscally conservative and prudent over the years, so we were not facing any financial difficulties. Still, as luck would have it, I was relieved and heartened by an email message from the CEO of the local hospital, Patrick Muldoon. Mr. Muldoon was a member of our Minority Coalition and seeking to expand participation and input from this segment of our community.

He wrote, "I have been meaning to contact you and express my admiration for your convictions. You are the most innovative chief of police that I have ever had the pleasure to work with." This meant the world to me at the time.

He invited me out to lunch and wanted to know if I would be interested in a short-term consulting position at Health Alliance Hospital in Leominster. We met shortly after, and I accepted a position as a consultant to review the security operations of the hospital and write a report on recommendations and best practices. This was a timely offer for employment for which I would forever be grateful.

Mr. Muldoon and the facilities manager, Dave Duncan, who would be my direct report, treated me with the highest level of professionalism and respect. I would soon learn how well this organization operated, and about the management leadership team and the teamwork that went into running a first-class hospital.

During the year I worked there, I was impressed with the humility and dedication exhibited by employees who truly put the patients first, above all other concerns. Whether it was walking a lost guest to a patient's room or taking the time to wash their hands 25 times a day, it was always, first and foremost, about delivering exceptional services. While I was there, the hospital received a high rating for cleanliness and was commended as one of the safest hospitals in the state for preventing the spreading of germs and infections to other patients.

As part of my review of security services at the hospital, I was clear in my conversations with my boss that I was not an experienced hospital security manager. He told me to visit as many hospitals as I liked to speak with other security directors and to compile a list of best practices to recommend moving forward. I traveled to many hospitals in Massachusetts, especially in the Boston area, and after several months, I delivered a 40-page report of recommendations to upgrade security.

The most sensitive part of the report was the need to upgrade security facilities and services in the emergency room for mental health patients. I underscored the fact that if this were not addressed, it would lead to serious civil liability. Management indicated that they were pleased with my report and would study it carefully. Unfortunately, I would learn later after I had left, that a situation had arisen exactly as I had predicted, and the hospital was held civilly liable.

This consultancy position led me to be offered the vacant position of Director of Security. In this role, I was responsible for two hospital campuses, one in Fitchburg and the other in Leominster. I was given exceptional trust and leeway to perform my duties and worked extremely hard to show my gratitude by training and encouraging the officers who worked for me to deliver the best services possible.

My first challenge was to raise the morale of the officers who had been leaderless for months. After working hands on with this small workforce of a dozen or so officers, I offered training, best practices and affirmation that resulted in a satisfied and willing security force. One example of the change in attitude was the installation of a time check-in clock to be punched at different locations at both hospitals. This system would provide recorded proof that officers were checking these locations on a consistent, regular, and yet varied basis.

When I had first taken over as the director, the officers scorned this idea and thought it draconian. By the time I left, they asked me to install this system so that they could prove their worth and efficiency to management. The atmosphere during the year I spent at Health Alliance was nothing but positive and affirming for me. It was not long before I would receive a phone call from a colleague with an intriguing offer to go back to work in the international field.

My friend, Bill Baker, who had done training on domestic violence for me in Russia called me and asked if I would be interested in working in Cairo, Egypt. He was part of a small, Washington, DC-based company that contracted with the U.S. State Department to hire a police advisor to work with the Egyptian Police at the American Embassy there.

I was surprised by this offer and could not fathom myself working in such an exotic place as Cairo. I thanked Bill for the offer but declined the position as being a little too far out of the box for me, then hung up the phone. I mentioned the position offer to my wife, Sue, and she was also surprised. I thought about it some more and realized that this was an international opportunity to use my skills in a different part of the world that I knew nothing about. Thinking further about it, this one-year position would give me time away from home and a chance to really process and grow from my intense experience as the chief of police in Fitchburg.

I approached my wife once again and told her that I had reconsidered Bill's offer and that I wanted to take the position. She generously went along with my decision and the sacrifice that it would entail with my being away. She was truly trying to support me in any way that she could. I called Bill back and told him that I was willing to take the position.

I was on an airplane to Washington, DC the next morning. I attended a meeting held at Bill's company office where I was briefed on the position and informed of my compensation package. Both conditions were acceptable to me, and I was off to Cairo in two weeks, after wrapping up loose ends at the hospital.

Touching down in Cairo on the runway was the beginning of one of the most extraordinary experiences of my life. When I was getting off the plane, I felt the strong, hot sun on my face and at the same time, inhaled a breath of polluted air that had a gasoline stench to it. This air pollution that I was experiencing for the first time was an everyday living condition for all who lived here. I was picked up in the airport lobby by a company-hired driver in his old Mercedes Benz. We then embarked on what I can only describe as a hair-raising and death-defying drag race on a packed highway for an hour until I was dropped off at the Hyatt Regency in downtown Cairo. The hotel would be a very comfortable accommodation for the next month until I could arrange for permanent housing. I slept the night away trying to somehow adjust to the seven-hour time difference and the laborious 14-hour trip to get to Cairo.

The Hyatt was a first-class hotel, and it was reflected in excellent accommodations, service and meals. Upon waking the next morning, I had breakfast and took a taxi to the embassy, located near the famous Tahir Square, a major political gathering point that could hold up to a million people when the need or crisis presented itself.

I was met at the embassy by the American police advisor that I was going to replace. I learned that the new U.S. Embassy was one of the largest in the world. It also became apparent that it was built after September 11, 2001, as the embassy was not approachable by anyone of hostile intent. Several layers of security were required for one to pass through before arriving inside. The building had walls 25 feet high extending into the air, giving the compound a look resembling a medieval castle. The building sent a clear message to those around that no one was to enter unless they were invited. Nothing short of a missile attack could succeed in breaking down the walls of this fortress.

After being processed, I was shown to the office where I would work, located in the basement of the building. I was told that it used to be a janitor's closet and that it had been cleared out to make a place for the contracted police advisor to work. It was an isolated working area that involved taking a ten-minute walk to find the next occupied office. It was then that Cliff, the gentleman I was replacing, told me, "Remember, you are not part of the direct U.S. State Department foreign service and as such, you are lower than whale shit."

Essentially, Cliff was telling me that I would be receiving no support from the embassy and that I was going to have to fend for myself while working in Egypt.

It turned out that he was basically right. After spending a month at the Hyatt Regency, I ended up taking Cliff's apartment when he left the country. It was in the downtown neighborhood of Zamalek, a short 10-minute taxi ride to the embassy.

Cairo is home to nearly 20 million people, maybe even more. No one is really sure. The main taxi vehicles were the ancient Russian-made Ladas, evidence of the years when Egypt was under Soviet influence. Not able to speak the language and with few locals who spoke English, I felt more isolated than I had ever felt before in my life. Going to a corner store to buy a quart of milk could be a challenge if you had to ask for it. I did quickly learn the phrase, *In Shalla* or "God willing," a phrase that seemed to be added onto every conversation.

I was on my own now. I managed to make a few non-State Department friends that included another contractor advising on banking, an Army Colonel from Boston who was head of U.S. Armed Forces in Egypt, and the FBI officer stationed at the embassy. All of them became good friends and people I could count on for socializing, but it wasn't long before I found out the real reason I was sent to Egypt as a police advisor.

I learned quickly that Egypt was a key ally of the United States in the Middle East. Home to a population of more than 50 million people, Egypt is the largest Arab Republic. Historically, Egypt had been mortal enemies with Israel and had suffered through two wars. When Jimmy Carter was president in 1978, he brokered a peace deal between the two countries known as the Camp David Accords. This agreement, led by Anwar Sadat of Egypt and Menachem Begin of Israel, brought a standing peace that has remained strong to this date.

My basic understanding of the agreement was that Israel and Egypt would receive financial aid each year from the United States. The money was appropriated for military aid in the amount of two billion dollars to Israel and one billion dollars to Egypt. Other components created trade agreements between the two former enemies. From a layperson's point of view, it was a peace that functioned, but came with certain costs. The agreement had brought about peace for the U.S. interests, Israel and Egypt.

There was one problem, however. For the U.S. government to legally give aid to a foreign country, it must adhere to what is called the Leahy Amendment. This legislation, named after Vermont U.S. Senator Patrick Leahy, states that the United States will not give aid to countries that violate human rights. It did not take long to see that the police, who had an astronomical rate of illiteracy, were very heavy-handed in their approach to policing, and that they violated human rights on a daily basis.

During the year I was in Egypt, the police I was there to advise never showed any willingness or desire to improve or alter their behavior. I was only able to meet with them three times. I offered them training courses that they showed no interest in hosting. I came to realize that my position represented to Congress an excuse to bypass violation of human rights for larger national security interests. I was placed there as an effort to show that the Egyptian police were trying. In reality, they had no interest in working with me unless I was willing to take a delegation to the United States. That was not going to happen, as the political advisors from the embassy informed me that the police were not interested in going to the states for training; instead, they were interested in a glorified shopping trip. In essence, my presence in Cairo was a complete joke.

I did have the opportunity to visit all the historic locations of Ancient Egypt in my free time and I will never forget the astonishing site of the Great Pyramids at Giza. Outside of tourism, I had learned some basic information about the Arab culture in Egypt. I found it to be a very interesting dichotomy. Religious attendance was fervent and massive at mosques during the calls for prayer throughout the day. But I also came to realize that there was so much poverty and bizarre places that I would never understand.

For example, outside the inner city of Cairo was a very large ancient Islamic cemetery from hundreds of years ago. Many of the tombs had small concrete buildings over them where families in the past would come to meet to honor their dead. This cemetery, referred to as the "City of the Dead," was occupied by thousands of people who lived there on a full-time basis. Riding by in a taxi, one could observe plentiful satellite dishes on these tiny buildings along with commercial advertising signs in the cemetery.

Another even more outlandish discovery was a place called Rubbish City. This was a region of Cairo that was home to Egypt's Coptic Christians. They were a break-off sect of the Roman Catholic Church and even had their own Pope. These Christians were discriminated against and were not free to travel safely in Egypt, and thus, congregated by the tens of thousands in this area. The main occupation of this population was to hand-sort the trash of the 20 million residents and repurpose and sell any salvageable items.

As you drew closer to this location, you could smell a strong stench of filth and garbage from several miles away. There were even paid tours offered by some companies to observe this living catastrophe. While visiting there, I learned of the cruelty inflicted on these people through frequent bombings of their churches and persecution and violence waged on them on a regular basis. During a breakout of the swine flu, local Arabs invaded the city and indiscriminately killed off many of their pigs, causing great economic hardship to these Christian people.

While there, I was surprised and moved when I was in a store and a man spoke to me in English. He said he was Christian, and he asked whether the U.S. government could please help them. I felt powerless to respond to this overwhelming holocaust of which little is known or talked about in the Western world. It was just another example of state sponsored discrimination and terrorism against these people which the official government did nothing about, totally ignoring violations of human rights.

One last situation I was made aware of was that Egypt had just received a squadron of American made fighter jets as part of their self-defense aid from the Camp David Accords. I was informed that Egypt, a country of more than 50 million people, was having great difficulty identifying capable pilots to fly these planes. I was subsequently told that one of the root causes of this problem was the state of hunger and gross malnutrition in the country, information based on a research study.

This reality combined with the massive amounts of illiteracy led me to understand why there was so much violence in the Middle East. I concluded that if people are not educated properly, if they suffer the severe effects of malnutrition on body and brain development, it is no wonder many of these people have resorted to violence so quickly to address their grievances.

I tried to maintain a healthy lifestyle off the job, and I joined a local choir who sang at the downtown Christian cathedral. It gave me the ability to socialize with English-speaking expats from other countries in Europe and enjoy an exercise that filled my time. One other remarkable highlight of my time in the Middle East was when my wife, Sue, came to visit me for a two-week stay.

I decided to surprise her by arranging a trip to Israel and the Holy Land. As both of us are practicing Catholics, we were excited to take in this experience. I was able to arrange a safe visit to Jerusalem through contacts at the U.S. Embassy. We stayed at a religious convent that was located just outside one of the gates of the Old City. We were hosted and guided by a wonderful and learned man who was a Christian Arab. Our stay was for two days, and we visited prosperous parts of Jerusalem and Israel. and all the major Christian holy sites.

It wasn't until we visited Bethlehem and crossed into Palestinian territory that we saw the other side of living in Israel. Entering this part of Israel entailed a thorough screening at a military checkpoint manned by Israeli soldiers. I couldn't help noticing how young many of these soldiers were. They were kids doing mandatory military service for their country. It was unforgettable to watch a young, teenage girl in uniform holding a large automatic weapon in a down position over her shoulder, pointed at the ground, as she searched our Palestinian guide.

I could see the anguish and humiliation on this man's face, a highly dignified scholar being searched by a girl who still looked like a child who probably had no understanding of the trauma and suffering she was inflicting on this man. This humiliation was visibly stated on a grand scale as we drove through the checkpoint and saw the enormous white concrete wall that separated these Palestinians from the Israelis. The presence of that wall screamed to me, "Keep Out! You are different and not wanted in our land." This was further emphasized to me when later in the day, my guide pointed out a highway in an open desert area that led to the Israeli settlements on the West Bank. I had learned of this aftermath of one of the wars and thought it was a rudimentary collection of housing. Instead, as I looked at the far-off settlement, I realized that it was a thriving small city.

It deeply disturbed me that Palestinians were not allowed to go there and were not even allowed to drive on the road that went to this settlement. These sights became imprinted on my brain forever. They would become increasingly disturbing to me as I witnessed the exultation and building of another wall and the racial rancor it would cause in the future in my own country.

After completing one year working as senior law enforcement advisor, I realized that, from a professional point of view, I was wasting my time and was caught up in politics way above my head. The Emergence Group and I mutually agreed that I would end working for them and return to the United States.

Chapter 16

My Stay at The Lodge: More Success for Fitchburg

Arriving back stateside, I felt a sense of relief to be free from American/Egyptian politics. Being home gave me the opportunity to reflect on my time in Egypt and some of the injustices that I saw. As someone who has prided himself on empowering those around me, regardless of gender, race, or background, what I struggled with most in Egypt was how they treated women. Being from the west, I could not fathom living in a country that did not acknowledge equality and the respect of women.

At the embassy in Cairo, there were constant reminders to staff, especially women, to be very careful when out in public. While I was there, an American woman was sexually assaulted on the street by a man. When the man was taken into custody, it was clear he suffered from mental illness. He had no way of getting his issues addressed, as services like these were not available to the poor. Thus, offenders like these were incarcerated for mental illness or put right back out on the street after serving time in jail.

When my wife and daughter were visiting me in Cairo, I made the mistake of allowing them to go to the famous bazaar by themselves. They had to leave there after being repeatedly verbally accosted. In plain English, this city was not safe for western women. This was further verified on the international stage after I left when U.S. News reporter, Lara Logan, was viciously raped in Tahir Square during the Arab Spring protests in the Middle East. These experiences only served to emphasize the importance of empowerment of women in all societies in order to build free and prosperous democracies.

With Egypt behind me, it was not long before the phone rang again. This time it was a fellow police officer, Tom Connell, who had participated in previous police exchange trips with me to Russia. He told me that his son owned a small technology business in nearby Gardner and was looking for a subject matter expert from the field of policing. He explained further that there were a couple of projects going on where my expertise would be valuable to developing software intended for use by police officers. As I had nothing else employing me at the time, I graciously agreed to meet with his son.

Within a day or so, I met with Tom Connell, Jr., the CEO and one of the most brilliant people I have ever met in my professional career. He explained his vision for public safety in the future. The company, Advanced Response Concepts (ARC), was in the process of creating a national identity card system that could be used by public safety personnel in police and fire departments.

Creating a database for fire personnel response was possible as they work on national standards. But this did not and could not work for police because each individual police department has its own set of policies and procedures. This process could be done on a department basis but could not be done on a national basis. This exercise also bore out the extreme complexities in trying to treat fire and police in the same way. Tom offered me a position at the company, and I accepted.

While employed with ARC, I served as a supervisor for a crew of engineers who were writing software for these products. Another project I worked on involved a hand-held investigative tool that could be used by police officers responding to calls and crimes which would help to more accurately document information and evidence. Although this was an excellent concept, the development of software to make this product accessible and usable by an average police officer was not completed while I worked there. After about a year, it seemed best that I move on from this position as I felt that working in technology was not something that inspired or interested me. It was also during this time period that I decided to take a one-year course to become a professional certified coach.

Helping others to succeed had been fulfilling for me throughout my career, whether it was an employee who worked for me or an unrelated client seeking advancement and clarity in their life or career. My research brought me to IPEC, the Institute for Professional Excellence in Coaching. The training took place over two semesters and involved learning techniques such as how to ask open-ended questions to guide clients to recognize their own goals and put a process together to achieve them. The training, plus hundreds upon hundreds of practice hours of coaching sessions with fellow classmates and people I knew in the community helped me to achieve my requirements for certification.

One principle that has always stayed with me was the concept of what a coach was not. A coach is not a therapist or answer person. My training instructed me to inform people about what coaching was not, how to recognize the signs if therapy or some other service was necessary for the client, and subsequently, how to refer the person out to a qualified individual. After completing my coach training, I decided to specialize in executive coaching for municipal leaders and police executives. I found the power of coaching others to be gratifying. It was a privilege to create and hold space for individuals to talk about their dreams, both professional and personal. Guiding them to achieve their goals through an inquisitive and self-reflecting process of questions and accountability was empowering to both the client and to me.

I had the fabulous opportunity to work with several police chiefs and municipal executives over the next two years. I found the work to be very challenging at times, but when a breakthrough occurred, it was the best feeling in the world. Many times, the key was to open a dialogue with a client so that they could give themselves permission to allow themselves to move forward. There was nothing I enjoyed more than watching others succeed.

I also managed to coach a few non-municipal clients along the way to reach their personal and career goals. That was how I met my co-author and editor of this book, Dayna Kendall. Dayna was a highly motivated fitness instructor whose classes I used to attend at the local gym on a regular basis. After one cycle class she asked about coaching, and we agreed to meet. I won't go into particulars, but she turned out to be one of the most highly successful clients I have ever had the privilege to coach, achieving all her goals.

On a lighter note, I also coached one of my favorite police officer friends, a woman of integrity, Linda Swears. I always enjoyed working with her and was appreciative of her skills and support during my time in Fitchburg. Linda opted for coaching to enhance her poker playing skills. I am pleased to say that today she is a fine poker play who travels the country to compete in tournaments at all different levels.

Although coaching was enjoyable, I found it difficult to create a full-time practice. There were many people who could have benefitted greatly from coaching but in the area where I lived, the income levels were generally not high enough for many clients to afford my services. In reality, the services that I offered were not expensive when one considered what was accomplished by taking on a coach to achieve one's goals. I was not able to generate the income that I was accustomed to and felt I deserved. I continued my coaching practice on a part-time basis.

It wasn't long before another opportunity arose to fill my time. More importantly, that opportunity allowed me to become part of something that would contribute to the success of my city and continue to build on the work that I had done as chief of police.

Great Wolf Lodge, one of America's best indoor water theme parks, decided to open in Fitchburg at a half-finished hotel located off a main highway that traversed the entire state. Under the leadership of

Mayor Lisa Wong, Fitchburg had attracted Great Wolf to choose the city over other New England locations with tax incentives that made the deal for both entities. The arrival of Great Wolf Lodge was the first good economic news that the city had received in a long time after a series of plant closings and businesses relocating away from the area.

As part of the project, Great Wolf expanded and modernized the hotel and built a beautiful, giant water park which employed many local contractors and created hundreds of new jobs, especially for youth in Fitchburg. After the deal was announced, I inevitably heard that most of the jobs that would be offered there were low paying and would not create long term wealth for the city.

Despite that knowledge, I saw the opening of Great Wolf Lodge as a godsend for our community. The arrival of this business was private industry's answer to address one of the two fundamental truths that our systems change task force had identified earlier as the root causes of crime in Fitchburg: systemic racism and lack of economic opportunity for at-risk youth. After being Chief of Police in the city and understanding how the community had been negatively impacted by drug abuse and violent crime, I knew that this new business could positively impact the youth in Fitchburg. I decided that I wanted to be part of this initiative to see that we did not take this opportunity for granted.

Great Wolf held several job fairs at their new location, hiring for all kinds of positions: lifeguards, desk clerks, housekeeping, restaurant workers, and security, among other company needs. I applied for a security position and was hired on the spot. I was impressed with the energy and positivity that the hiring staff exuded and the enormous amount of young people representing a true cross section of our youth who were eventually hired to fill these positions. It reminded me of the first job that I got when I was fifteen years old.

I had applied at McDonalds and had lied about my age to get hired. They finally dismissed me after I kept forgetting to bring in my work authorization card to prove that I was sixteen years old. The good news was that when I turned sixteen a month later and I was immediately rehired. McDonald's was a minimum wage job. I started at $1.65 an hour.

What I remember most about this job that has helped me succeed later in life were three things. First, it instilled in me the discipline of work for the first time. My personal time was no longer my priority. Arriving to work on time and doing a good job was first. I once received a whopping $5 bonus for being the fastest worker on the floor during the lunch time rush.

Second, the training that I received about the history of the corporation impressed me. The corporation's success seemed centered on the philosophy of consistency and professionalism. The food was always prepared properly and, more importantly, I was trained in the manner of how to cordially welcome and service our customers, starting with saying, "Welcome to McDonalds, how may I help you?" I later used this same cordial approach successfully throughout my career.

Third, I learned the importance of teamwork. The atmosphere of this workplace promoted team members to rely on and support each other. Whether it was a manager who made sure that I had a ride to or from work, or one taking the time to encourage and affirm me, that job experience had started me off on a career of professionalism.

What was really exciting to me was that I saw this same philosophy of consistency and professionalism employed and enhanced at Great Wolf Lodge. Hundreds of teenagers of all backgrounds and races were hired to work for the company. All the employees were repeatedly trained in customer service and teamwork. The company went so far as to regularly sponsor events for their young employees that rewarded and enhanced their teamwork, improved their individual skills, especially around customer service, and utilized a system of affirmation and promotion for continued success.

I know that Great Wolf Lodge was not necessarily a career job for most of these young people, but it provided an opportunity for many of them to start off life on the right foot and to build on these principles throughout life. Great Wolf was a safe place within the city where all were treated equally when they walked in the door. Sure, it was a nationwide chain, but little things like national corporate executives coming out to visit Fitchburg and washing employees' cars in the parking lot was a visible example of humility and leadership not lost on my eyes nor on the eyes of others.

My time at Great Wolf was a very positive experience for me. I had the chance to be part of a renaissance for Fitchburg and to observe hundreds of healthy young people productively employed and growing in self-esteem and worth. At the same time, this company and these young people were restoring a sense of value for our city. Working security at Great Wolf, I had an intimate look at how well this company was run. Whether it was in caring for the customers or by providing impeccable cleanliness to its guests in the hotel and water park, a new culture of success had been created in Fitchburg.

Amazingly, it would not be uncommon to recognize professional athletes and their families from the New England Patriots to the Boston Red Sox coming out to enjoy a first-class experience of rest and fun. Seeing this success and having the opportunity to work with, coach, and mentor these youth, I was able to see the application of wonderful resources to continue systemic change and opportunity in our community.

After about a year and a half with Great Wolf Lodge, I received a phone call that would once again call me to the international arena. It was from the U.S. State Department asking whether I would be interested in applying for a position working directly for them as a Senior Police Advisor at the U.S. Embassy in Chisinau, Moldova. Moldova was a small Eastern European country with a population of three million people, roughly the size of Maryland, and was strategically located between Ukraine and Romania. I was eventually interviewed over the phone by officials from the U.S. Embassy and Washington, DC, and was ultimately selected for and offered the position.

Anxious to embark on a new learning journey, I appreciated that, in this position, I would be working directly for the U.S. State Department, but that meant I was required to go through Secret Security clearance. This turned out to be a long, drawn-out, and exhaustive process that took over nine months to complete. I embarked on a preliminary trip to Moldova for two weeks during the clearance waiting period and stayed at a local modern hotel in the downtown district. This trip allowed me to meet my future fellow employees and to get a feel for the job and the capital city of Chisinau. All systems were in place for a successful beginning.

Chapter 17

Moldovan Life and Politics: Proving Myself Again!

It was mid-June of 2016 when my wife, Sue, accompanied me on my formal arrival to Chisinau, Moldova. We landed at the local airport, a tiny and antiquated facility with no formal gates and quickly deplaned from our 727 directly onto the runway, then loaded into a bus. After a short ride, we were soon delivered to a door leading to customs. We shuffled into a short line and came before a customs officer who examined our passports. He did not speak English and we did not speak his native Romanian language, but fortunately our U.S. Diplomatic Passports allowed us to be ushered through quickly to pick up our luggage.

Entering the main lobby of the airport, we were greeted by my boss and director of International Narcotics and Law Enforcement (INL) in Moldova, Don Carroll. He drove us twenty miles to our comfortable and generous U.S. Embassy-provided house, one that I would be living in for the next three years. Then, it was onto the embassy to be formally introduced to my new staff.

Arriving in downtown Chisinau, I was surprised to see an older classical building that once housed a small theater and now featured a hodgepodge of unsightly additions. The original footprint of the property had been expanded due to a demand for workspace and to ensure the safety and security for those working there. I quickly learned that the vast majority of employees who worked at the embassy were Moldovan citizens. This included people such as Alex Molcean, our senior Moldovan law enforcement specialist at the U.S. Embassy, who would quickly become my partner and loyal interlocutor with the police. He, like so many other Moldovans, was the backbone and institutional memory of the embassy.

These employees did all the administrative work that allowed the Embassy to interact with the Moldovan government in a productive and professional manner, offering services ranging from translation and interpreting to influencing politics that strengthened the mutual relations between our countries and furthered the cause of democratic growth in Moldova. From a logistical point of view, I found out immediately that my working office would not be located at the main embassy campus, but up the street at what was probably the nicest building in the city, a large, multi-floor, classical Romanesque building fronted with large ionic stone columns.

The International Narcotics and Law Enforcement (INL) and the Media and Public Relations departments functioned separately from the main headquarters. INL was the division of the State Department that worked with foreign countries who were trying to modernize their police practices and reform to a more democratic style of policing. I would be the senior police advisor working to make this happen.

I always felt fortunate that I was able to work in the modern and spacious, more comfortable office space instead of the crammed and outdated main headquarters. Adding to the pleasant workspace that I would occupy was the fact that my new office was just a brisk 20-minute walk from my house.

After all the other experiences I had in the various countries where I had worked, the house I was assigned to live in was both a relief and a luxury. It was a nicely furnished, three-bedroom house in a good neighborhood where many diplomatic families lived. The property was gated with beautiful gardens and a full garage. Although I ended up getting a car, I appreciated the convenience of living so close to my work. If I was in a hurry, for five cents I could even take an electric streetcar that ran almost directly from my neighborhood to my workplace.

Sue was invaluable to me, helping to set up the house after our shipment of personal items had arrived from back home. She would be my strong support during my service there and would periodically travel back and forth from the United States to stay with me for several weeks at a time, giving up working in her highly successful business back home, Susan Cronin Draperies.

I was now a resident of Chisinau, the capital city of Moldova, with a population of about 600,000 people, roughly the size of Boston. My role seemed fairly clear to me when I arrived at my new assignment. I was here to advise both the American and Moldovan governments on how to progress from a controlling, Soviet militia-style police force to a western, democratic police force whose primary purpose was to serve its people.

My first task was to get to know the people I would work for and with. I was immediately embraced by my foreign service officer supervisor, Don Carroll, the gentleman who had picked me up from the airport on my first day and who had quickly arranged for me to buy a solid old Toyota RAV 4 from a departing American military officer. This was a huge help that facilitated my ability to get around the city and to have access to supplies and services that I would need throughout my stay in Moldova. Don introduced me to our Moldovan staff who warmly embraced me. We were tasked with the critical job of helping this country to grow into a democracy.

The second task, and what would turn out to be the most challenging part of my work in this country, was learning the hierarchy, politics, and personalities of the people who ran the U.S. Embassy. Unlike my experience in Egypt, I did not feel a stiff arm pushing me out of the way, the ever-present reminder that I was not needed or wanted there. Instead, I learned from my supervisor that Moldova was politically deemed a "captured state" by the American government. It was a country that was granted independence after the breakup of the Soviet Union in 1991. This had resulted in a strong division within the country between those who had allegiance to Russia and others who were more western leaning.

Since gaining independence after the fall of the Soviet Union in 1991, there had been several elected governments in Moldova, representing both the former

Communist government and advocates of democracy. Moldova, being the poorest and most vulnerable country in Europe, and located in a strategic area between Ukraine and Romania, was and is a very important state and symbol of influence between the major democratic countries of the west and the future influence of Russian propagandist policies.

In 1990, a section of Moldova decided to break away and become an independent state aligning with Russia. Subsequently, a war broke out between Moldova, Moldovan separatists, and Russia that resulted in the Russian-occupied breakaway area known as Transnistria. Although it has succeeded in breaking away and it harbors Russian peacekeepers, it does not have international recognition as a sovereign, independent state.

In some sense, Moldova is a continuation of the effects of the Cold War. Even though the conflict had officially ended, the reality was that Moldova still felt the real effects of the Soviet influence and the coercion of the Cold War powers. Sadly, this political instability was further complicated by the endemic corruption of oligarchs who had seized government power for profit. Most of this corruption, based on an intricate system of bribery, was just a continuation of government practices under the old Soviet system that claimed to be fair to all, but instead abused and cheated its citizens of growth and prosperity for the benefit of corrupt elites. During the time I was in Moldova over $2 billion dollars disappeared from the government, representing 15% of the GDP of the poorest country in Europe.

Upon learning about the recent political history, I was introduced to the hierarchy at the U.S. Embassy where I was told that Moldova was, indeed, a "captured state" which is basically understood as illicit control of the state for personal gain by corporations, the military, politicians, and others, through the corruption of public officials.

My new colleagues informed me that the police and courts were so corrupt that if those at the Embassy had a choice, the money provided to INL would be funneled instead into women's programs. I immediately suggested a couple of ideas on training for the police and was quickly and forcefully rebuked. Upon hearing their response, I asked, "What do you want me to do?"

The answer to me was, "I don't know." Needless to say, this meeting and others like it became very intense and confrontational. I explained to my superiors that having served as a police chief in the United States, I was accustomed to being questioned and having my performance reviewed. I understood the need to closely monitor what INL and I did while working in this politically sensitive country. However, these repeated tense meetings were not doing anyone any good. It got to the point where I would call our weekly meetings at the embassy our weekly beating.

One week, when I was unable to attend one of the weekly meetings, I spoke with one of my colleagues at INL and asked him how his weekly beating went. He looked at me with tears in his eyes and walked away, acting as faithful as he could, in order to avoid maligning his superiors, but at the same time, being obviously personally humiliated for his efforts.

I was disturbed by how this whole process emotionally impacted everyone involved. After finally having a basic idea of where I stood, I knew I had a big challenge on my hands. I had been hired to work as a police advisor to bring the democratic process to a country steeped in corruption, while being frowned upon for my efforts by the embassy staff.

When I would eat in the embassy cafeteria, the topic of work was widely avoided, and I would occasionally catch a smirk at me when the other person thought I was not looking. The message sent was, "You are naïve, and you don't belong here."

Faced with this seemingly impossible task of trying to do what was right while still pleasing my employer, I decided to implement the only strategy that I knew. I was determined to be forthright and honest in all my efforts and to build relationships with coworkers and with those around me, in order to establish trust to bring about change. I was fortunate to work with several Moldovan colleagues in my office who introduced me to the police and to many of the agencies they worked with.

Alex Molcean and Anatoli Popa were my interlocutors working directly with the police. I was also assisted greatly by INL employees Tatiana Lungu and Ludmila Avtutova connecting me to all the agencies working on domestic violence with police. As fate would have it, right about the time I started working, a new police chief for the country was appointed. It wasn't long before Alex Molcean and I were introducing ourselves in the office of Alexander Pinzari, a towering, athletic and handsome six-foot-five individual with a giant smile who only seemed to grow taller when he rose from his chair to shake my hand. We had a polite introductory conversation followed by a pledge to establish a cooperative relationship that could benefit the people of Moldova and the policies of the United States government. Chief Pinzari was taking over for the prior chief who was widely considered to be corrupt. Whether Chief Pinzari was "a good guy" or not, he inherited the aura of being corrupt, having been appointed by the same administration.

My boss at INL was open to me learning the ropes and suggested that I visit the country of Georgia where a highly developed and successful program of police reform had been established, led by a U.S. police advisor from outside the State Department. I took advantage of the opportunity and within a couple of weeks, I was in the capital city of Tblisi, Georgia, meeting with him and his staff and listening to their advice.

I witnessed the profound changes that had occurred in Georgia since the firing of the whole police department and a new process put in place to replace them with honest and professional police officers. I certainly was not in a position to make these kinds of changes overnight, but I did come away with a firm and solid understanding of where I had to start. I learned that it was essential to identify good and reliable police officers and to begin training them. But as I was told, "Get them the hell out of there and bring them to the United States to let them learn and observe in a free, supportive and professional environment."

I began my work by proposing that a select, small, influential group of police officers from Moldova, including the new police chief, accompany me to the United States to attend the International Association of Chiefs of Police (IACP) Conference in San Diego, California. Having attended this annual conference on multiple occasions, I believed this venue to be the perfect place to create professional and personal relationships with my new Moldovan colleagues. Past experience had taught me that they would be exposed to the best and most innovative practices of modern democratic policing that were being embraced by the best police departments in the world. This was the very same conference that I had invited my Deputy Chief from Gardner to attend with me.

I knew the impact that this learning opportunity could afford to police personnel at any level. Attending this conference would also expose my Moldovan team to a three-day trade show featuring the best of technology and equipment available today. Even though these police were coming from a cash-poor country, I believed it was more important for them to see what advancements existed to steer their mindset toward progress and away from corruption.

The police officers we elected to take to the conference were living the harsh reality of corruption that was firmly ingrained to draw all ranks into a negative reinforcing cycle. Police officers on average made a salary of about $100 dollars a month, an absolutely deplorable wage that could not possibly sustain an employee and their family. This lack of a livable wage created what I observed to be a mafia-style, capo regime.

As impossible as it was to live on a salary of $100 per month, advancement had its own price tag, I quickly learned. Approximately 40 regional chief of police positions existed throughout the country. There was no system for promotion. Instead, it was rumored that the price for "buying" one of these positions was 40,000 Euros or $50,000 US dollars. Once the position was procured, lower ranks in the police were expected to pay tribute to their supervisors. When a common police officer would do a traffic stop for speeding, they would inform the driver that they were going to get a ticket and a fine of approximately $50.00. The driver would then be given the option to pay $25.00 with no record of court appearance. If the driver paid on the spot, they went on their way, after getting the fine cut in half. That money did not go into the system; instead, a portion of the collected fine would be paid up to the next level supervisor and so on until ultimately the chief of police would get a cut.

Because the system received no funds in the process, this corrupt practice held a vice-like grip on policing in Moldova and ultimately cost the police the trust of its citizens. When I started working in the country, the Moldovan Police had less than a 20% favorability rating with people and extremely low trust that was measured in several independent polls sponsored by the U.S. Embassy. This kind of corruption was present in all aspects of their society from any kind of government services to the medical and education fields. It was ghastly and unthinkable to me.

After deciding to bring this group to the U.S., I proposed it to my boss who seemed surprised and yet open to the idea. I later met with high level officials at the embassy and presented my idea. I was immediately grilled and told that the embassy would not support a big party and shopping trip to the United States. I understood the hierarchy's cynicism, seeing this trip as a perk to some of the high-ranking police officials rather than what it was intended to produce. Instead of trying to defend my ideas for professional development, I took their inquiry as a personal insult to my profession.

For years in the United States, policing had fought to be recognized as professional and had undergone years of education and training to raise performance levels based on solid data and proven research. I was extremely proud of the work that I had done in my career based on what I had learned at the conferences in the past. I immediately took the response as a slap in the face to policing everywhere and stated my strong objections to their response, explaining that it reflected a biased and uninformed view of modern-day policing. Ultimately, I was granted the authorization to take the new chief and a small group that year to the conference being held in San Diego, California.

    I met with Chief Pinzari and explained the structure of the conference to him. I told him that when I had gone in the past, I would always take my wife with me, paying for her expenses out of pocket and not relying on public funding for her to join me. Taking family with me and seeing other chiefs doing the same created a strong bond of professionalism among the attendees and gave us a sense that we were like any other executive officer in the world. We could manage to have a terrific professional experience while creating social bonds to promote all our future efforts, built on deepening our trust and relationships.

    In October of 2016, we were off to San Diego, California, for the IACP conference. Due to our late registration, we were not able to get a hotel near the convention center where the show was being held. Instead, we booked a hotel right on the ocean ten minutes from downtown for half the price of a downtown hotel. The vast expanse of California and the Pacific Ocean had the unintended effect of mesmerizing my Moldovan colleagues who came from a tiny landlocked Eastern European country.

I rented a ten-passenger van and drove the group to the conference center in the morning to confirm their registrations and to give them an orientation. Upon arriving, I made it a point to go around the vehicle and open the doors for my guests. Sue and I made extra efforts to check in constantly with our group to ensure that they were acclimating well to their destination and experience. The first goal of bringing the group to the U.S. was to create trust and form a cohesive learning unit. By attending to both their personal and professional needs, we soon began to form a bond that resulted in the group attending seminars, learning new concepts, and creating a general sense of excitement of what could be rather than what was happening back in their country.

At one point, when we were walking back from lunch to enter the center, the Moldovan police chief noticed a small phalanx of uniformed bicycle patrol officers who were positioned to tactically keep the area clear and safe for crowd control. These conferences are high profile, and it was not unusual for different groups to show up and protest the conference. He was impressed that the presence of bike patrol officers was a great way to offer a non-threatening police presence while allowing officers to interact with people in a friendly and effective manner while maintaining crowd control and public safety.

Chief Pinzari turned to me and asked, "Ed, what would you think about forming a bike patrol in Moldova?"

I was surprised by his question and as we were just at the beginning of our training, I responded that we could talk about it later. I appreciated his insight but honestly felt a bit dismissive of the suggestion. It was later that I put together the practicality of his requests as Chisinau had experienced violent crowds and police protest confrontations that usually featured police dressed in riot gear with clubs and armor. Chief Pinzari was already envisioning the use of non-threatening bike units as an alternative to the heavily armed and equipped police the next time there were protests at home.

The conference was intense and passed quickly. The show was five days long, featuring hundreds of cutting-edge seminars on police and law enforcement policy, methodology, and technology. We attended as many presentations as we could and were strongly supported by our Moldovan interpreter who was part of our group. Our attendees were given expense money for their meals and other incidentals. Instead of leaving them during these times, we all would take our meals together and continued to express our views and learn about each other. At one point when we were walking into a restaurant to eat lunch, I noticed several American servicemen in uniform walking ahead of me. I quickly walked ahead of this small group and opened the door for them and thanked them for their service to our country.

Chief Pinzari immediately exclaimed, "Yes, Ed! That is how I want people in my country to respond to my police officers!" You can't anticipate these kinds of learning experiences until they happen, but it only served to affirm how important it was for our Moldovan officer to see an interaction like that, one that demonstrated trust and admiration from a member of the public to our servicemen; that these soldiers were being given this encouragement and affirmation because they had earned it.

CHAPTER 18

The Plan and the Mission: From Corruption to Success!

Prior to my arrival in Moldova, I had researched and reviewed the work that my predecessors had done with the Moldovan Police departments. The advisor whom I was replacing had improved police training in special tactics, had built a modern forensic laboratory, and developed plans to build a new shooting range. While conducting my research, I located a study sponsored by the U.S. Embassy to overhaul and reform the Moldovan police.

The report was quite innovative and highlighted ways to eliminate corruption, promote women in policing, and switch to community policing methods, among other recommendations. The study was so comprehensive that it was later used as a model for the European Union and their massive $50 million initiative to completely overhaul and physically renovate the whole infrastructure of the police throughout the country. Surprisingly, a new community policing station was just being completed with U.S. funding.

One of my first tasks was to advise and implement a community policing program that was meaningful and sustainable to the Moldovan people. I also reviewed many U.S. sponsored polls and documents that asked people what they saw as the most important services that police could provide. They had identified lack of supervision of young people leading to crime, and general cleanliness in their neighborhoods that created a sense of fear of crime and a poor quality of life. Interestingly, the topic of domestic violence had been identified as a huge problem and was borne out by the amount of time police spent on these calls and issues.

The new community police station in Chisinau did not resemble what we know community police stations to look like in the West. Opening a new community police station in Moldova had no resemblance to this Western model. Moldova has very little violent crime. All firearms and their forensic traces and imprints are tested and registered with the police. There are no gang problems, and virtually no discrimination with the exception of the recognizable practice of distrust towards the *Roma*. (The *Roma* people commonly referred to inappropriately as gypsies are a nomadic people present in Europe and are often excluded and looked down on.) People in general had no fear of walking on the streets at any time of day. The new community policing station, a converted department store, had a wide glass facade lending the idea of transparency to the outside world.

After returning to Moldova from the IACP conference, Chief Pinzari and I were able to benefit from the trusting relationship we had established during our time together in California. We shared many conversations. When communicating with him, I cited instances where I had made mistakes as a police chief during my career and how I had learned from these mistakes to bring about safe and effective policing. I have always felt that all police officers are human and want to do the right thing. Teaching from a method of failure and success adds an element of humility and opens the door for honest conversation to bring about real results. I think the Chief was surprised by my frankness and it helped to create a sense of openness and risk taking that would lead to further success.

When the new community police station was set to open, I suggested to Chief Pinzari that they address a well-known but unseen problem in Moldova: domestic violence. Having worked in other countries of the former Soviet Union, I had witnessed societies that have evolved differently from the west in terms of women's rights. Domestic violence seemed to be widespread throughout this region and it was no different in Moldova. Most of these Eastern European countries practice, or at least follow, Eastern Orthodox religious traditions that insist that families stay together even if abuse is present in a relationship. This unfortunate dynamic appeared to result in huge unintended consequences for women in Moldova. Domestic abuse did not allow for these women to prosper or to help the economic development of the nation.

I suggested that some of the space in the new station be offered to a non-governmental domestic abuse advocate who could provide services for women in a confidential manner. Chief Pinzari enthusiastically responded, "Yes, Ed! That's a great idea!"

This idea was implemented and put in place and was highly effective. The advocate assigned was from the NGO LaStrada, led by their co-directors Ana Revenco and Daniella Misail-Nichitin with whom INL had developed strong ties and trust. At first, the police were reluctant to have a civilian working in their police station, but when the advocate was able to address difficult issues in these cases, they gladly welcomed the assistance. As a side note, Ana Revenco would become the future Minister of Internal Affairs for the country and Daniella Misail-Nichitin would also take on a high-level position of trust in the government. These women would come to power after the election of the first woman president in Moldova, Maia Sandu, a Harvard graduate backed by the U.S. government.

This service and programming at the new community police center was an affirmation of the trust building and commitment that was built after our visit to the IACP conference in San Diego. It was the first program to bring direct services to the people of Moldova. It was starting to pay huge dividends that brought real services to a large population of women. The long-term effects of this type of programming in countries where women have been restricted empowers women to grow with the economy and encourages positive uncorrupted efforts and energies to bring about real long-term change, as demonstrated above. I have been, and will always be, in agreement with the honorable Kofi Annan of the United Nations who stated that the "empowerment of women was the greatest tool for developing a nation".

Following up on working with the police by incorporating a strong woman's NGO that provided meaningful services to its citizens, I was encouraged to promote women working in the police department. Moldova, like other countries of the former Soviet Union, employed female police in primarily administrative positions. Modern day policing allows women to fully participate in all areas of police work. Mainstream training that includes women police officers was essential to building their skills and bringing them into leadership positions. Because most of the women police officers I met held no power positions, I deduced that most were not involved in corruption and would be an ideal place to provide support and resources to bring honest non-corrupt changes in the police.

Soon the opportunity to test this theory presented itself. While co-presenting a training session on systems thinking and policing with my colleague and subject matter expert, Dr. Carol Sharicz, I met Cristina Schimbov. At 37, Cristina was a 19-year veteran and senior investigative officer of the Moldovan police. During a break, Cristina introduced herself to me. I was immediately impressed with her English language ability, her intelligence, and her inquisitive nature. It soon became clear to me that she was an exceptional police officer.

About that time, I met with the FBI representative for Moldova who was visiting from his station in Romania. During our discussions, he mentioned to me that he was looking for a candidate from Moldova to attend the prestigious FBI National Police Academy. This was a three-month course presented by the FBI in Quantico, Virginia, that emphasized executive development. Ideal candidates were mid-career police officers who were rising in rank or had potential to rise even further. More importantly, the officer invited to attend had to undergo a thorough background check and a record of integrity in their service. The FBI invited exceptional police officers from foreign countries to not only add to their professional capabilities but also to develop strong international connections that could be used in the future to assist in international investigations.

I soon met with my FBI representative and nominated Cristina. After passing the application and background investigation, she was invited to attend. A few months later, she completed the National Academy Session 273, and was the first female police officer from Moldova to graduate. Cristina brought credit upon herself excelling at the Academy, but more importantly to me, she also represented the untapped resources of women in leadership positions in the Moldovan police. She would go on to become the founding President of the Women's Police Association, an uplifting organization strongly supported by the US government, European Union and the Swedish National Police. This organization has been developing women of integrity in leadership positions in Moldova since then and has been trained in state-of-the-art Western police standards and in all areas of women's empowerment. Most importantly, in Cristina's words, "The support has promoted democracy, true democracy" in Moldova.

During the rest of the time I spent working in Moldova, I had the opportunity to develop deep professional and personal relationships with Chief Pinzari and my European colleagues and advisors. My house became the unofficial meeting place for planning and making decisions on future endeavors. My wife, Sue, a natural host, who has taught me so much about affirming and supporting others, was key to this success.

We hosted regular dinners and celebrations at our house that truly deepened our trust and understanding of each other's goals and mission. During these meetings, I met the European representative for police reform in Moldova, Steven Daniels, a former Belgian police officer who had become a talented diplomat. These opportunities allowed me to develop a strong and lasting relationship with chief superintendent and reform project manager from Sweden, Ulrica Grandberg, one of the most talented police officers I have had the pleasure to work with in my career.

This relationship also gave me the opportunity to travel to Sweden with a delegation of Moldovan police officers, including Chief Pinzari. I sat in on the trainings being taught by seasoned Swedish police officers. I was impressed by their presentations. Two incidents stood out during this trip for me. First, during a training session that emphasized how to work and listen to people rather than telling people what to do, Chief Pinzari openly exclaimed, "That is how we should have been trained to begin with," casting doubt on the still Soviet-style police training in place at the present time in Moldova.

Later on in the week, our group visited a community center in Stockholm for teenage youth. The purpose of bringing the Moldovan police officers was to show them how Swedish police would meet informally with youth in the community to listen and respond to their concerns, especially at times when no crisis was present. This afforded Swedish officers to develop trust and bonds for the future with these youths. During this visit, we observed a Swedish Police officer sitting at a table with several teenagers, listening intently to their concerns. One of the teens had a bright head of orange hair. I could only imagine what the chief was thinking, coming from his conservative country.

After completion of our training visit to Sweden, Chief Pinzari invited me and our EU colleague and Swedish advisor to a conference where he addressed all 40 of the Moldovan national police chiefs under his command. He presented community policing methodology to his chiefs and announced that this would be their model of policing moving forward. He even took a moment to tell the group about the orange haired youth and that they and he would also listen to people like this.

My relationship with Chief Pinzari continued to blossom. On one memorable occasion, the chief invited my wife and I and visiting family members to a horse ranch. I was presented with a beautiful stallion, adorned in American symbols on his hoofs, to ride that day. Although I had no real interest in riding, I assented after the chief took a few laps around the arena on this magnificent animal, conjuring up images of Moldova's ancient patriarch and founder Stephan the Great.

When he finished his ride, I ended up mounting this powerful animal, but to my horror, the horse threw me. I ended up breaking seven ribs and was quickly transported to a modern hospital in Chisinau where I recuperated for the next five days.

Every day that I was in the hospital, the chief's assistant, Stefan, would visit me in the morning and bring me a cappuccino. This sounds like a little favor, but it meant the world to me that they cared about me and showed it with this small gesture of support and sincerity. As a leader, I have always tried to be there for my people. When I was a police chief, when any event affected my officers, I would show up and personally make sure that they were okay. Whether it was sitting with an officer's family suffering from a personal tragedy or carrying out from his home the deceased body of an officer who had died of cancer, being present at these crucial times were and are imperative to creating trust.

The trust building with the Moldovan Police continued to the point where I asked if they would be interested in the U.S. Embassy bringing in the number one police reformer, Khatia Dekanoidze, in Eastern Europe to assist in their reform efforts. Khatia is a Georgian who had played a key role in reforming the police in Georgia after the breakup of the Soviet Union. She had worked closely with the U.S. and was able to help lead an effort that totally reformed the Georgian police and eliminated corruption. She was later hired in Ukraine to be the National Police Chief of the country and started a similar reform effort there.

As soon as I suggested this idea to the chief in his office, he rose from his chair behind his desk and said, "Yes! I have tried to reach her for some time without any success."

With the chief in agreement with this proposal, we brought Khatia to Moldova a short while later. I had the opportunity to work closely with her over the next few months. I have never met a more dedicated and non-corrupt police official in Eastern Europe in all my career. I asked the chief to allow Khatia to work at his headquarters and he readily agreed. I also asked if I could have an office there and he enthusiastically said yes. I didn't realize that this last request would have dire consequences to my future work in Moldova. In the meantime, we continued to implement community policing programs in Moldova, including the first police bike patrol units.

We brought in trainers from the U.S. who did a great job and were well received by the Moldovan officers. This effort brought the bike officers out into the local parks and community and in contact with people. It was also a refreshing role for officers who had very little job satisfaction because they were not paid well. In a twist of fate, the first unit of 12 officers that we trained resulted in a woman police officer being made the supervisor of the unit.

Around this time, I received an email from our deputy chief of mission, who had been formerly extremely skeptical of any efforts to work with the police. The message was a compliment to me. It said that I was doing a great job and that it was her understanding that the Moldovan police had our trust to the point where they would check in with us before beginning any new ventures. This email came out of the blue as I no longer attended embassy meetings for INL, but it was satisfying that we had won over the hearts of both the police and our own embassy leaders.

In the two trips that I had taken officers from Moldova to the United States, I was able to introduce them to the concept of a Family Justice Center. This concept was new to me at the time as I had been out of mainstream policing in the U.S. for a few years. A Family Justice Center is a "one stop shopping" type of place where victims of abuse and domestic violence could go to receive help. In Boston, the unit came under the jurisdiction of the Department of Public Health.

Many police officers worked out of this independent building along with social workers. The main idea of the unit was to allow a victim to reach out for help and tell their story one time. Upon telling their story to a caseworker, the caseworker would identify the needs of the victim that could range from need for employment, enrolling children in school, or finding adequate housing. The police worked closely with all of these non-governmental agencies to provide appropriate services for victims, and in doing so, created trust and the ability to provide meaningful and sustainable changes in victims' lives.

I saw this as a model that would address the most pressing problem facing the Moldovan police: domestic violence. By empowering women in the country to break the cycle of abuse, the center would contribute to national development and at the same time, satisfy embassy leadership's goal of creating a valid and worthy project to support the police and the people of Moldova.

I eventually met with my bosses at the embassy and proposed the idea. I think when I first suggested the project, I startled some people. I explained the project and simply asked, "Will you support a Family Justice Center in Moldova?"

After a short period of silence, the response was positive. As a result, embassy leadership participated in a study visit to Fort Worth, Texas, for a National Conference on Family Justice Centers that was attended by various representatives of the Moldovan government, ranging from the police to judicial and public health areas. The trip to the U.S. went extremely well and upon our return to Moldova, I was informed that the embassy had allocated almost $1 million dollars to support the project. This project is still in the development stage but is happening as this book is being written. It is one of my proudest achievements from the time I worked in Moldova.

Despite all of these positives that were taking place, I received a call from Khatia from police headquarters that she had been called into the chief's office. He instructed her to leave the building immediately. This all came about because I was planning on putting my office next to hers and the chief's, and the U.S. Embassy safety rules dictate that I had an explosion-proof door installed. I was told that a corrupt governmental official noticed the construction on the door and was informed that Khatia and I were working in the building.

Khatia was immediately kicked out of the building, and later on that evening, I received a threatening message through Facebook Messenger that I was "going to get hurt." Upon receiving this message, I met with the chief and informed him I could no longer work with his government. I told him that I knew that he was not responsible for these actions, but it was impossible to move forward at this point. After almost three years of working on police reform and promoting much progress, I had hit the heart of corruption, and corruption was pushing back. It was time for me to go home.

The story does not end there. Since I left, the Moldovan people have elected a female president. Many women were recently brought into key political positions and Moldova seems finally to be moving in the right direction toward true democracy.

I believe the work that was done with the police to institute and promote democratic policing and empowerment of women had strong and lasting effects. The country is now led by a brilliant young woman who has hired two of the best women in Moldova to work in her administration; those women had been strong non-corrupt allies of the U.S. Embassy and national patriots.

In light of the Russian invasion of Ukraine in 2022, I think that the work to strengthen the Moldovan government and assist in democratic changes is more important now than ever. Moldova is at risk of a Russian invasion after Ukraine, but they are now stalwart defenders of freedom and a strong ally of the United States and Europe. Moldova is resolved to become a permanent member of the European Union and its standards of free and democratic government.

CHAPTER 19

Just Police Reforms: History Tells Us So!

Having devoted a career to professional law enforcement, I have been fortunate to see policing done in many different countries and in many different ways. One conclusion I reached is that the key to successful policing is building personal relationships and trust with the people you are working for and with, and that the best use of power is to give it away to others, allowing them to grow and become strong. Working with others is the best way to true sustainable change and success.

Policing should be a constant and evolving process that responds to the needs of its constituents and is constantly learning to adjust its methods for the betterment of their communities.

I believe that recent events centered around the issues of Black Lives Matter and the subsequent attacks on police practices highlighted by the recent George Floyd and other shootings of people of color are not surprising.

Policing has been in existence for centuries, dating back to ancient times when military elements were called upon to protect the rights of the state and individual citizens. It was not until the founding of the London Metropolitan Police led by Sir Robert Peel in the 1820s that policing as we know it today was created. Any student of criminal justice is familiar with this milestone of progress remembered in the phrase, "The police are the people and the people are the police." The police are only effective when they have the consent of the people they serve.

The old form of military style policing was cruel and ineffective. Prior to the creation of a modern police force, it was common for civil disturbance to break out in the cities of the United Kingdom. When things got bad enough, the military would send in troops to battle with and remove trouble-makers to the extent that the military and its methods were hated and resented by the people.

Sir Robert Peel changed the role of police from an enforcement model to a servant model. As a visual representation of this, the police now wore blue uniforms instead of military red. They changed the buttons on their uniforms from shining brass to copper as a deliberate attempt to de-escalate the appearance of police as oppressors and to become a new organization of service, with the objective to create trust with the citizens they served.

In the history of our 250-year-old republic, the police have been misused to enforce the wrongs of our founding fathers in acceptance of the institution of slavery, our original sin. They were used to enforce the laws of slavery, and even after emancipation, police were again misused to reestablish laws of suppression against minorities' rights. This was not a southern or regional occurrence in our history. Rather, it was a modern-day acknowledgement that displacement of native American people and the expansion of slavery was a joint effort of both the northern and southern sections of our country. This joint effort proliferated the growth and profit of cotton that was the 19th century equivalent to our current use of oil as a driving economic force.

At its roots, American policing was assigned the task of treating the minority elements of our society differently and reinforcing the wrongs placed upon them since our founding. It is a history that American society has brought to bear and unfortunately which still has dire effects today. The recent shootings of Black individuals by the police and the advent of Black Lives Matters is just a continuation of the basic injustice of the imperfections of our establishment as a country.

My analogy is in no way meant to be a criticism of the men and women of law enforcement in our country today, but rather a recognition that they are playing the role that society wants them to play.

I believe that the police could be a change agent for our country. Rather than "circling the wagons" in defense of our profession, we should take the bold steps of examining our history and lead a change in society for equality and ultimately a much stronger and more prosperous society.

This short historical analysis demonstrates that over the centuries of civilization, policing in its present-day basic form is barely 200 years old. As I write this summary, I would point out that the development of "modern policing" is still in its infancy. I have endeavored to challenge the status quo and call for a revamping of our policing and police training in America, not because police are wrong, but because we can be much more effective at serving our people and strengthening our democracy.

To that end, I will conclude this book with thoughts on what policing might look like in the future. As a practitioner of systems analysis, I believe that before we can change policing there needs to be an honest reflection conducted by those in the field. They must ask themselves the questions I asked myself as chief in Fitchburg - "How do we make the problem worse? How do we as leaders consciously or unconsciously make the problem worse?" This seems counterintuitive, as it implies that we are part of the problem. But no change will come about unless we make a concerted effort at honesty not only by looking into our practices, but by accepting the facts that we can do much better in service to our communities and to our profession.

I would also argue that overcoming the inertia of law enforcement is a daunting task, particularly in America, where it is a well-established and funded institution. Policing was once a profession that was based on brute force and poor wages. Our police officers today are, for the most part, well compensated and educated to the point where standards and policies have brought a level of professionalism to an all-time high. I would support all these efforts in moving policing forward, but I do believe that despite all these great efforts, the key to "Just Policing" is not in policies, procedures, or legislative reform. Instead, it is in the wisdom of honestly examining the results of law enforcement and violence in society today and acknowledging that we can and must do much better.

As hurtful and tragic as these incidents are both to communities of color and to the police themselves, I believe that this erosion of trust has been accelerated in the last twenty years, beginning with the events of 9/11.

Prior to September of 2001, policing in America had undergone a renaissance through the more elevated practices of community policing. This program, funded by the Clinton Administration and the Department of Justice, was originally intended to put 100,000 new cops on the street. As part of this initiative, money was allocated to hire police officers and to train them in community policing. The effect of this program was to create a new policing culture that encouraged police to work closely with their communities. As a result of this practice, many innovative and promising strategies were created by police and the cities that they served. It also had the effect of creating trust between police and communities of color.

There was also a dark side to the increase in funding for police and that was the advent of programs like zero tolerance that reduced crime, but had a negative impact, fueling the mass incarceration of people of color that we are still dealing with today. In fact, America incarcerates more people today per capita than other western countries.

Because of fear of more terrorist attacks, police funding was replaced by enhancing and expanding resources for national security. A whole new branch of government was created for this purpose: Homeland Security.

To further complicate the situation, America was drawn into two protracted wars in the Middle East that drained trillions of dollars to support military operations that were aimed at defeating terrorists abroad who had attacked us. As a result of these wars, two policing change influencers emerged: One, policing no longer had funding for building community programs, and two, many young people who had served in these military operations over the last twenty years were leaving the military and joining policing.

As I have said here previously, veterans of the military make fine police officers. I do, however, worry that bringing many new war-involved people into the policing profession also has resulted in regressing into a more militaristic style of policing in the United States. One can easily see the results of normalizing the use of armored police vehicles and dressing in combat gear on the street; it has now become commonplace.

An unintended effect of our country's reaction to homeland security, terrorism, and wars has been to diminish the importance of working with minority groups, and subsequently, has resulted in a lack of trust between the police and these parties. Crisis situations have been exacerbated in recent times because of the absence of the continuing building of trust. As a result, when there is a police shooting for instance, there is no bank of trust to draw from, and instead, there are national protests and violent reactions from offended communities. Likewise, the police are put on the defensive for what they believe and what many of those in white America believe as "just doing their job." The fallout in many communities in America has resulted in the call to "defund the police!"

From my point of view, I believe that in most of the police shootings in question, the police were only doing what they had been trained to do. Also, there were and will always be situations where police make mistakes and people tragically are killed as a result. I think what is missing in many of these situations is an honest, trusting, developed relationship between police and communities of color.

Building that strong relationship before more events occur is part of the answer. Creating that bank of trust to draw from and refer to can give consent for police to do their job. Unfortunately, in many of these communities, no bank of trust had previously been created to help explain and rectify police action in times of crisis.

The U.S. has a population of just over 330 million people and incarcerates over 2 million people (.6%), while China has a population of 1.4 billion (over four times the population of the U.S.) yet it incarcerates only 1.6 million (.1%). How do those numbers validate the claim that our criminal system is just, fair and effective when, by percentages, our incarceration rate is six times per capita that of China? I am not implying that the police are responsible for these figures. I believe that the basic unaddressed history of our country's treatment of our minority groups is responsible for the imbalances and exclusions in our society today and that the police are only doing the job they are trained and asked to do.

When we face calcified problems of crime and violence in our cities today, no amount of policy change will significantly impact the status quo. Instead, we must realize that the roots of this violent phenomena are not in policing, but in society in general, admitting that we are still living in an era of a divided and unequal society that continues to deny true opportunity, prosperity and democracy to all.

The key is to change the relationship of our law enforcement personnel to the people we serve. This can be done through a change of heart, a true shift and commitment to understanding of the plight, history and circumstances of our minority population. This can be accomplished by employing training in deep listening skills, community engagement and restorative justice. We are capable of understanding the experience of helplessness of people who are excluded from fully participating in society without feeling attacked. We can respond with methods that bring true justice and healing for crime victims and perpetrators.

I would also strongly support the use of restorative justice practices in policing, as opposed to employing only traditional methods of arrest and bringing suspects to court and trial. The results of our criminal justice system are currently a disaster. Even when a person is lawfully arrested and brought to court, there is nothing in the process that really helps the victims. The court system in our country is adversarial and punitive in nature, and mostly results in victims dissatisfied with the process and offenders reacting with a high level of recidivism. Restorative practices can also serve to reintegrate offenders into society later and initiate a true rehabilitative effect.

Recent work done in schools in the United States using restorative practice tools such as talking circles and harm conferencing have proven highly effective in reducing out of school suspensions and repeat offending, especially by students of color who were being disciplined at a much higher rate than white students.

Only when the police open their hearts and work with our communities will we gain the trust and the consent of our people. These changes will allow a truly honest discussion of the reasons why crime occurs and what truly can be done to address it in a fair and just manner.

Unless we have the courage to look at the roots of systemic racism and oppression, we will never begin to end the inequities of our unconscious society. One way to address these deep problems is to educate ourselves and our children on the main faults of our founding as a nation. This does not mean that the values, traditions, accomplishments and hope generated by our nation for over 250 years are wrong. Abraham Lincoln called America, "... the last great hope of earth." As in both Lincoln's time and in our own Civil War, we are called to understand and absorb the pains of our mistakes, admit our faults, and work intently and personally with historically excluded people to bring about a true and just society.

Likewise, our training of police officers also needs to be changed. Components of our academy training should include allowing recruits to intermingle and work with members of our society who live in our troubled neighborhoods and are victims themselves. History has taught us that although police can be called to suppress violence and use deadly force, the vast majority of policing time is spent in working and talking with people. Practices that encourage and develop conversations and trust with our people are one key to reducing crime. This is one area where police have gotten it right in the past.

Moving forward, I would like to see an honest, scientific assessment of the services that police provide today. This would involve the type of experimentation that is going on in some of our cities today. We all decry the call to "defund the police," but I think the call is actually a request for the police to adjust their services in a way that brings them closer to the people. I would like to see police consider the reallocation of resources as we did when I worked in Fitchburg. Why not use confiscated drug money to fund jobs for at risk youth to address crime instead of increasing the amount of search warrants?

We know today that mental illness has been widely ignored in this country and that a large segment of people that the police are called to serve are suffering from these issues. Why not hire professionals in these areas to work with people who need these services instead of dispatching fully armed police to address these issues? In doing so, consider a change in uniform for these professionals that sends a totally different message than the present-day police appearance sends.

My summary of the concept of Just Policing lies in this single statement: Policing is and should be a constant and evolving process that listens to the changing needs of its constituents and is constantly learning to adjust its methods for the betterment of their communities.

I know that many of these suggestions I have offered will seem Utopian and naive to many modern-day police officers and their leadership. But I would offer this: If we apply changes that result in trust from our communities, we will be much more effective in our service, reduce crime, and create a more just and fair society.

\# \# \#

About Edward F. Cronin

Ed Cronin has worked in the law enforcement field for over 35 years. His career includes experience as a Police Chief in two cities in Massachusetts. He holds a graduate degree in Criminal Justice Management along with an advanced graduate degree in Organizational Development and Systems Thinking from Suffolk University.

As a Detective Sergeant with 15 years' experience, he took courses at Queen's College in Oxford, University, England as part of his master's program at the University of Massachusetts at Lowell. During this time, he also worked with the Thames Valley Police in London, exposing him to new ideas and methods of policing practices. He later participated in bringing the first group of U.S. police officers to Russia after the fall of the Soviet Union in the early 1990's, a venture that was featured on national television in the U.S. This trip was followed by the first Russian delegation of police officers to come to the United States, eventually meeting with then-FBI Director Louis Freeh and subsequent meetings with the U.S. State Department who agreed to fund future delegations to the U.S.

While acting in his first Chief's position in Gardner, Massachusetts, Ed co-created a highly competitive grant application that resulted in an award from the U.S. Department of Justice using an innovative community approach to combat domestic violence.

After three years in Gardner, Ed was hired by a Vermont-based International NGO, called Project Harmony. He was appointed as Director of a U.S. State Department funding program called Domestic Violence Community Partnership Program to the countries of Russia, Ukraine, and Georgia that was based on the model he had used in Gardner, Massachusetts.

In 2006, as Chief of Police in Fitchburg, Massachusetts, he co-developed a task force that employed a systems approach to address crime and educational failures of Latino students. Fitchburg was experiencing a higher murder rate per capita than the city of Boston (mostly within the Latino community) and a high school dropout rate for Latino students of over 40%. His ground-breaking work brought the police, the minority community, and the greater community at large together to engage in a process that identified the root causes as systemic racism that was mostly unconscious, as well as a lack of economic opportunities for at-risk youth. This work resulted in Ed receiving the 2011 Individual Achievement Award in Civil Rights from the International Chiefs of Police.

This effort by Ed and the team he created refocused the community to address these deep-seated issues that eventually brought about systemic and political change. Today the City of Fitchburg has experienced a Latino dropout rate of less than 8% (down from 40%) and only one murder in 2021.

Ed also has extensive international experience, having worked in Cairo, Egypt, at the U.S. Embassy as a police advisor and three years as Senior Police Advisor to the police of the country of Moldova in Eastern Europe. While working there, he assisted in bringing democratic policing practices and empowerment of women that has assisted in the formation of a strong Western-leaning government. This work has been magnified in importance in light of recent Russian aggression toward Ukraine and other former Soviet republics, including Moldova.

About Dayna Kendall

Dayna M. Kendall serves as the Restorative Justice Interventionist in the Ayer Shirley Regional School District in central Massachusetts. Previously, Dayna worked in middle and high school education, serving as both a classroom teacher and a school administrator. Dayna holds a bachelor's degree in Government and International Relations from Clark University, a Master of Arts Degree in Teaching English from Fitchburg State University, and a Master of Education in Education Administration. She is currently working to obtain her Master of Science in Restorative Practices from the International Institute for Restorative Practices in Bethlehem, Pennsylvania. Dayna lives with her husband and two sons in Leominster, Massachusetts.